GETTING IT

A GUIDE TO UNDERSTANDING AND APPRECIATING ART

BECKY HENDRICK

Custom Publishing Editor: Cyndi Eller
Custom Publishing Production Manager: Kathleen McCourt

Library of Congress Catalog Card Number: 00-103005

Printed in the United States of America.

ISBN: 0-618-06671-3
3-98277

1 2 3 4 5 6 7 8 9 - DS - 02 01 00

 Houghton Mifflin
Custom Publishing

222 Berkeley Street • Boston, MA 02116

Address all correspondence and order information to the above address.

CONTENTS

INTRODUCTION

Several years ago the local community college asked me to teach a course in Art Appreciation to students who were majoring in anything except art. Simple, I thought. Since I have been a practicing artist for nearly thirty years, since art consumes my day-to-day life, and since I love talking about it --- particularly to a captive audience --- what could be easier?

Then I looked through the textbook --- 500-plus pages and several pounds of information about art's purposes, history, media and techniques --- and the challenge became clear and daunting: make the enormous subject of art meaningful to students whose ages range from eighteen to eighty, with diverse life experiences and goals, and whose attitudes toward art run the gamut from mild interest to outright hostility. And one other thing: accomplish this in less than forty-five hours!

Putting together the curriculum for Art Appreciation classes taught me the value of the adage that the best way to learn about something is to teach it. It occurred to me early on that wise students (and instructors) absorb the data, dates, facts, examples and minutiae in order to discover lessons within the wealth of information. And it is those lessons, rather than the facts that lead to them, that we take with us into the world. If the lessons are valuable and meaningful, the world outside the classroom and areas beyond art will validate and reinforce them. In the Art Appreciation class I teach and in these chapters which the course has inspired, I have chosen to focus on the general lessons that art teaches us and to supplement those lessons with enough examples to illustrate and prove them.

As I continue to fiddle with the curriculum, trying and erring, deciding what to leave in and what to leave out, I consistently conclude that there are only two requirements for appreciating art: we need to look at art objectively and without prejudice; and we need enough information about art's relationship to history and culture to support our non-judgmental explorations. These may be simple goals, but they are not necessarily easy ones. They are the goals of this book.

Getting It is not intended to be a textbook. There are many wonderful Art Appreciation texts that provide extensive visual examples and details that this volume does not include. Since words about art are inadequate without illustrations, and since many of the words refer to artists and their art, you will be well served to have illustrated textbooks or art history books on hand. Rather than being a substitute for any textbook, *Getting It* is meant to replace the instructor, to replace me!

The essays are arranged like the course I teach: sequential, cumulative, with gradual and increasing momentum, the early chapters provide a basis for subsequent ideas and more complex concepts. A complete reading, from front to back, will provide a thorough 'course' in Art Appreciation, but the book can also be read in a piece-meal fashion to refresh and illuminate certain topics of interest.

As I write this, I am more and more aware of the differences between my life experiences, education and skills and those of my students, many of whom were born after 1980. Conditioned by the digital age, by fast-forward, cell phones and Velcro, they are often prepared for the high-tech future at the expense of knowledge about the past. Since my audience, in a classroom or in a book, spans all ages and backgrounds, I play it safe and take very little for granted. Consequently, some readers may find certain topics covered in the following chapters to be unnecessary while others may find the information new and relevant. A little review of history? An elementary lesson in color? It can't hurt.

Now, an admission. When I was first asked to teach Art Appreciation to non-art majors, I was slightly offended. I am a serious artist. I have taught serious art to serious students at serious institutions for two decades. Once I got over the silliness of outward appearances --- *how will this look on my resume?* --- I discovered that teaching about art in a fundamental way required me to consider the subject in a profoundly holistic manner. And, to be perfectly honest, this course has proven to be the most rewarding assignment of a long and diverse teaching career. It never fails me. If I begin a day tired and discouraged, I leave the lecture hall reinvigorated, with renewed spirit. It is never boring, never routine, and never, ever harmful.

A student sent me a letter at semester's end that said, "This course should be called *Life* Appreciation!," and she was right. The lessons, no matter how basic or how many times I repeat them, are not only art lessons, they are life lessons. And no matter how elementary the subject matter is, it affirms the most positive aspects of human experience. Instead of burnout, I get enthused all over again. Teaching Art Appreciation has been and continues to be a most welcomed, life-enhancing gift which I am happy to pass along to you.

PART ONE

OPEN EYES, OPEN MINDS

CHAPTER ONE

BEGINNING

Open any picture book dealing with important art of the last century and you will see a painting by Jackson Pollock. *That's just paint thrown around...* you might say; *my child could do that.* Or you witness long lines outside a major museum, with people patiently waiting to see an exhibition of Piet Mondrian's paintings. *Such simple shapes,* you think; *what's the big deal? What's the point?*

We just want to Get It.
We have eyes, we have brains.
Don't we have a *right* to Get It?

Imagine that art --- *serious* art, the stuff that's hard to Get --- is hidden behind a closed door, high on a hill. Between us and it lies a broad field, a gap filled with all manner of obstacles: false myths and misconceptions, incomplete information and misinformation, prejudices and preferences stand in our way. Before we can begin to explore the lessons that art offers us, we need to clear away some of the impediments that block our path.

The first obstacle is the word itself: Art.

The Word...

How to begin talking about art? The word is so big that it is used to include just about everything that can be done at a high level of expertise: cooking is called art; so is Wall Street deal making; jewelry, clothes, furniture are labeled as art. And the people who do all these things are described as artists: there are tattoo artists and graffiti artists. Everything can be called art and whoever does whatever it is can be called an artist.

A stranger approached me at a cocktail party. *You're the artist?* she asked; *My son is an artist.* Making social chit-chat, I responded, *Really? What kind of work does your son do?* And she replied, *Oh, he's only eight years old!*

Poor artists. If child's play is considered to be art, should we consider what artists do to be the equal of child's play? Let me be clear from the start: what this volume addresses is *not* something done for fun, as a hobby or diversion. The art of the museums and art history books is exclusive, and some of the things it excludes are:
    things done for pleasure, leisure, and self-expression
    things done for interior decoration or accessories
    things done to advertise a product
    things done for therapy
    and things done for money, fame, tenure or other external rewards

Sure, it's possible for artmaking to be therapeutic or pleasurable; on occasion art is rewarded by a sale or by recognition; it can hang on a wall or fill a space in a decorative and pleasing way. But make no mistake, the art that this book deals with is not an adjective: art therapy is valuable as therapy, not art; commercial art is business; art education serves educational goals more often than aesthetic ones. The art of the museums and history books is different: rather than being created in response to external demands, it is *internally* motivated. It is worth serious consideration; it is significant; it matters. It is art with a capital A. Pronounced in a reverent tone, we pause slightly to signify its importance: head raised, a quick inhale and it's ... *Art.*

To complicate things, art is also *inclusive.* At its highest and most exclusive level (--- *Art* ---), it includes work that is pretty, ugly, or neither. It includes work made of precious materials and traditional art media (paint, marble, bronze) or of surprising, unorthodox and experimental materials (earth, light, even a urinal). It sometimes displays careful drawing, painting and craftsmanship, but it can disregard technique altogether. Art can take a lot of time and effort. Or not: it can be a spontaneous, effortless creation (based, of course, on all the work that came before). Some art can withstand centuries and millennia, and some is temporary and transitory.

Art can be *representational*, with subject matter related to the visual world. It can be *abstract*, with identifiable subject matter that is intentionally distorted, simplified or altered in any number of ways. It can also be *non-objective*, with lines, shapes and colors presented as lines, shapes and colors, not 'about' anything outside art's own formal language. Art can be overtly political; its subject matter can be troubling or provocative. It can be of the utmost seriousness or it can make us laugh. Art includes work of a highly personal nature, or it can be theoretical, intellectual, and universal.

None of these characteristics --- prettiness or ugliness, subject matter, materials, skill --- are the reason a particular work is considered to be High Art It may help to think of art as an active force and the art object --- the painting, sculpture, installation or performance --- as the manifestation of that force. The art of the museums and history books *functions* as Art.

Art works...

"That isn't art..." I hear people say this all the time.

I wonder why we so often expect art to conform to a narrow definition with fixed characteristics, while we are open to the wide-ranging possibilities of music. We know that some music is intended to make us dance, some evokes rapturous praise, and other music moves us to be very still and quiet. We sing to it, dance, hum, pray, salute, march and make love, and we consider it all to be music.

Visual art, too, is multi-purposed, functioning in varied and numerous ways. And its functions are always evolving. Long before organized religion and science, art was a way to appeal to forces outside one's control; it functioned as magic. Before the invention of the printing press, art instructed. Before photography, art recorded events. Art's functions change, along with its materials and intention, in relation to the world which brings it into being.

Art matters. It has the potential to 'work,' to affect the artist and the world. It participates in the evolution of ideas.

> *Art is one way that truth happens. In art, truth is in the work. Art is one among a number of ways in which truth establishes itself --- political creation, religion, sacrifice, thinking. Truth is unconcealment, the revelation of the being of what is.* (Heidegger)

And the artist --- the Artist --- who works at this rarified level is motivated from within to seek the "revelation of the being of what is."

It makes me nervous to use a term like *truth*, bandied as it is from talk-radio microphones, and to presume that we all agree on a single definition. I use the word as carpenters do: when the board is straight and aligned in all directions, the bubble in the carpentry level is centered, and the board is 'true.'

Artists don't go into the studio crying out *Truth, oh truth, where are you?* and few of them would be comfortable expressing their intentions with such elevated terminology. Instead, if they can describe their goals at all --- art is a non-verbal language, and some of its practitioners claim inarticulateness as a virtue --- artists might address the particular intentions of a specific work: its formal issues, its relation to an idea or event in the culture, its source. Jenny Holzer might describe the intention of her work to be the consideration of the anonymous voice of authority; Cindy Sherman might allude to the gender-politics of representation; Brice Marden might refer to his paintings as a continuation of Modernist formalism, exploring spatial ambiguity. Like building a pyramid, individual artworks often function like the building's foundation or a low level of stone, but all great art (literature, music, philosophy, etc.) reaches toward the point, toward that which is true.

> *You take something that is important to you, something you have brooded about. You try to see it as clearly as you can, and to fix it in a transferable equivalent. All you want in the finished print is the clean statement of the lens, which is yourself, on the subject that has been absorbing your attention. Sure it's autobiography. Sure, it's fiction. Either way, if you have done it right, it's true.*
> (Wallace Stegner)

Perhaps it is that kernel of truth imbedded deep within great art --- what the ancient Greeks called 'the divine center' --- that insinuates to us art's value and suggests that there's something worth "getting," even if we don't yet know what it is.

'Getting' it...

When we look at art, particularly art that is new to us, unfamiliar and sometimes confusing, we want to figure it out, to connect with its significance and meaning. Art is a visual language; seeing something that doesn't match anything we've seen before is like hearing a foreign language for the first time. How can those sounds mean anything? How can anyone understand it? And in art, how can those lines, colors, shapes and materials mean anything? How can *I* understand it?

> *If you do not understand a man who speaks a language you do not speak, is this therefore proof that the man babbles only nonsense?*
> (Hans Hoffman)

It's understandable that some people, faced with Modernist and Postmodern art that is complex and confounding, might be led to one of two conclusions: that art is a joke, and the joke is on them; or that, with enough time and effort, knowledge and faith (faith in museums and authorities, artists and Art itself), something of real value will be revealed.

It isn't a joke.

We want a key to unlock art's meaning, a map to help us reach its point, a way to break its code. We want to Get It, to understand what the work is about and why it is considered to be important. That is the *content* of art: its point, its significance, its function, its subject or theme, what it's 'about' in the largest sense. The problem is that in art, in great art, content is not visible; it doesn't announce itself, and it isn't easy to detect. When we look at a work of art, we don't see its content, we see its form. Form, in the words of artist Ben Shahn, is "the shape of content." While content is idea and essence, form is material and tangible. Content is the fuel; form is the vehicle. Form is the way art moves us toward meaning.

> *The more the proportion of emphasis on 'idea' and 'form' approaches a state of equilibrium, the more eloquently will the work reveal what is called 'content.' Content, as opposed to subject matter, is that which a work betrays but does not parade.*
> (Erwin Panofsky)

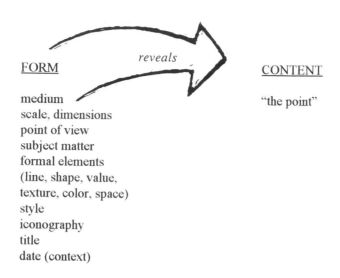

FORM   *reveals*   CONTENT

medium   "the point"
scale, dimensions
point of view
subject matter
formal elements
(line, shape, value,
texture, color, space)
style
iconography
title
date (context)

The artist enters the studio with an idea. Thousands of choices follow; some of them are deliberate and conscious ones, while others are intuitive; some 'just happen.' Like a chemist working in a laboratory, the artist confronts the sum of all the elements and their potential combinations. The scientist doesn't arrive at a discovery by arbitrarily mixing any and all of the chemical elements. The artist, too, limits the possibilities, choosing certain elements and combining them in relationships that serve the content of the work.

> *I thrust forward into space as science and the rest do. At a time when experimentation expresses itself in all forms of life, search becomes the only valid expression of the spirit.* (Mark Tobey)

CHAPTER TWO

PREREQUISITES

Trite but true: we know what we like. Sometimes our personal preferences, our likes and dislikes, can create obstacles to understanding art and appreciating it. Years ago I came across an interesting exercise (in *A Life of One's Own*, Joanna Field's essays on writing which is long out of print) that addresses the subject. Don't let the simplicity of this activity deter you; this exercise can change your life, and I commend it to you.

Divide a page into two vertical columns, one headed with a plus sign (+) and the other with a minus (-). Under the '+,' list whatever comes to mind that you really, really like: foods, movies, clothes, vacation spots, people, things to do, anything. Under the minus sign, list anything and everything you can think of that you strongly dislike: foods, personality types, t.v. shows, it doesn't matter. This is a private exercise that you never have to share with anyone, so you are free to be totally honest, and to make mistakes.

This simple activity creates a mental file and programs your mind to pay attention to your involuntary responses as they occur in the world, to be objective about your subjectivity. Since beginning such a 'file' ten years ago, I've continued to add to my initial list which started out as a record of rather trivial and unimportant items. As I go about my daily routine and encounter something that makes me think or even say our loud " I *hate* that!" or "I *love* when that happens!," I add it to my list. If you pursue this exercise for months or years, the things that move you to strong reactions --- personal responses that are individualized, spontaneous, unpredictable and therefore authentic --- can be wonderful tools for self-discovery. When we become aware of our honest, unprogrammed likes and dislikes, we can in little but significant ways begin to shape our lives to give us more opportunities for the 'plus side.'

(Since classroom teaching has cured me of self-consciousness and pride, I'll reveal a few recent items from my 'likes' list in order to make a point. I really like it when I'm parked at a traffic light, and the turn signal on the car in front of me is blinking in time to the music on *my* radio! I love picking up a random number of things --- paper clips, toothpicks, papers --- for a given task and having the number turn out to be the exact one I need! I love making significant eye-contact with babies in stores, glancing at a digital clock and having it read 11:11, and clothes with pockets. And I *hate* people talking during movies; cell phones in restaurants, films, classes, and *church*!; being told something --- car repair, doctor's visit --- will take X minutes when they know it will take Y.

See how personalized these revelations can become? Cheaper and more convenient than psychoanalysis, they can help you make decisions and structure a routine which will limit the negatives. For me it means making choices that give me plenty of solitary time, time for 'magic' moments to occur, and developing strategies for avoiding unnecessary interruptions. I don't hesitate to *hush* loud-mouthed movie-goers. And I shop for pockets.)

Our personal preferences are important to us as we look at art, but once again they help us learn about ourselves, and that is altogether different from learning about the art. The trick/skill is to be attentive to our subjective responses to different artworks and to learn about ourselves by discovering our preferences, but to keep our likes and dislikes separate and flexible. Our individual tastes can change over time.

I was raised in a quintessential family of the fifties; with an emphasis on good behavior and manners, we never raised our voices in anger. No wonder this particular incident stands out. As young adults, my sister and I discussed the film *Annie Hall* at a family dinner. "It's a terrible movie," she declared, and I, who *became* Annie Hall for days after seeing the film (five times), screamed with trembling anger and unprecedented wisdom, "You can say you hated it, but you can't say it is a bad movie!" Too often we see a work of art and we say *That's great!* when we actually mean *I like it!*, or we think *Terrible!* instead of *I don't like it.* Those are the times that our likes and dislikes become obstacles that can interfere with our Getting It.

Prejudice can get in the way, too. In the opening chapters of *Art: The Way It Is*, author John Adams Richardson presents a brilliant illustration of prejudice that goes like this: each of the four vertical columns of numerals listed below is arranged in a meaningful and significant way. None of them is random or arbitrary. See if you can make sense of each one; see if you are able to Get It.

A	B	C	D
0	0	3	8
1	2	7	5
2	4	9	4
3	6	1	9
4	8	4	1
5	1	6	7
6	3	5	6
7	5	5	3
8	7	2	2
9	9	8	0

Row A is obviously arranged in numerical order; B presents sequences of even and odd numbers; in row C, each subsequent pair adds up to 10. Row D is more problematic. Give up?

Surprise! Row D is arranged in alphabetical order. Eight, five, four, nine, one, etc...

Here is the lesson: it is almost impossible to understand the reasoning behind row D because it doesn't conform to what we expect. Numerals are most often related to counting or mathematics, and since our expectations are shaped by what we know and experience, we try to force the arrangement of symbols to fit our preconceived notions. No matter how hard we try, we will never be able to penetrate the mystery of row D with arithmetic; if we insist on using that key, we'll never unlock the door to its meaning. We'll never Get It.

We sometimes respond to art in a similar way. Bringing the wrong set of expectations to any work of art is like using the wrong key. If you expect all numerals to work like A, B, and C, you'll never get D; if you expect all art to be pretty or technically correct (or ugly and difficult), if you expect all paintings to be pictures (or to be non-pictorial) or all sculptures to be statues (or not), you will be locked out of understanding a lot of art.

I remember the first time I heard rap music pulsing out of a teenager's earphones from the back seat of a cross-country trip. Silly me, I thought music had to be something hummable, and as I cranked up the volume on a golden-oldies station, I thought and probably said *That's not music!* Now, years later, rap music has its own category for a Grammy award, and even old coots like I can recognize the brilliance of Snoop Dogg.

Prejudice is sneaky. It doesn't announce itself: *This is the voice of prejudice speaking.* Instead, it is subtle, speaking in a soft internal voice and manifesting itself in body language: a shrug, a facial grimace, a scornful scowl, a 'raspberry.' Our prejudicial voice says "that's *just* some paint thrown around...," "*that* isn't art," "that's *only*..." "*pfttt!*" Each of us has to learn to recognize our own personal biases as they occur, in thoughts, gestures and attitudes, and resist them: *TIME OUT!*

And what are some of the typical prejudices toward art? We tend to be biased toward what we are familiar with, what we like. So prejudices toward art tend to suggest that art is better when it's pretty and well-crafted; that artworks using precious materials are superior to those made of base media; that art that takes a lot of time and effort is more valuable than works that 'happen' quickly; that certain subject matter is preferable to others; that art *should be* --- insert words here --- realistic, precious, emotional, personal, impersonal, rational.

The problem is that none of these categories of art determine the greatness of any particular artwork or any one artist. Certainly, making sense of art would be easier if one category, one set of rules, or a single criterion fit all, just as it would be easier if it were nothing more than a matter of taste, *just* each person's opinion. But like anything of real importance, it isn't that simple. And it turns out that it is the very complexity and contradictions of art that make the effort to Get It worthwhile and satisfying.

It takes time...

Someone --- a doctoral student, I'll bet --- computed that the average time spent looking at a work of art in a museum is ten seconds. Ten seconds! That's probably just enough time to glance at the art and to decide whether it appeals to us personally, to pass judgment on it and to walk away. Doesn't it seem odd that someone wanting to Get It would pass judgment on art as a first step rather than a final one? Because that's what judgment is: closure. We know this; in a court of law, after all the evidence is heard and all the arguments are made, a verdict comes. The judge pounds the gavel, and *case closed*. Judging, whether it's done in a courtroom or in a museum, is the last thing we need to do, if in fact we need to do it at all.

Who does need to judge art? Artists certainly do, since judgment *is* the process of artmaking. Every decision is a form of evaluation and, as the work progresses, so does judgment. *Is it working?* the artist asks; *Is it complete? Should I add, delete, reconsider? Is it worth keeping, or should I abandon it and begin again?* Museum curators judge as they select artworks and exhibitions for their institutions and audiences; art teachers pass judgment by awarding grades to student work; gallery owners evaluate art in relation to their clients' needs and the marketplace; art critics and writers judge art in order to make sense of it for their readers.

That leaves out most of us, and yet judgment is often the first thing we bring to the experience of looking at art, and sometimes it is the only thing. It isn't judging that is so harmful, it's *pre*-judging --- assigning value based on our personal preferences and inadequate information: *prejudice*. We like to think that artists, curators, teachers and writers make their judgment calls without prejudice and from a position of experience, knowledge and objectivity, and the good ones do.

    Art is high on a hill, hidden from easy understanding by a locked door. We try to eliminate the obstacles in our way, and we search for the right key. If we are attentive to our personal preferences and prejudices, we can postpone judgment and keep our minds and hearts open to art's varied and inclusive possibilities. The door opens enough to reveal a thin shaft of light, evidence that something valuable and illuminating lies behind it. When we separate our subjective reactions and suspend our judgment, we create a wedge that holds the door open to possible understanding and appreciation. We've got a foot in the door. And the wedge? It's the Big Toe of Faith!

CHAPTER THREE

ART AND EYE

Once you've taken care of the preliminaries --- your judgment is on hold, your preferences are in their useful place, your mind is open --- you can look at art with an objective eye. The best way I've found to connect with what an artist is doing and what an artwork is doing is to describe the work of art objectively, without interpretation or analysis, without speculation or presumption. Simply describe what you see using neutral, value-free terms.

Describing the forms in front of you requires you to spend minutes, rather than seconds, engaging with the art and looking at it in an objective way. Since objectivity and subjectivity are mutually exclusive states of mind, it is equally important to be spending some minutes *not* being subjective. Objectivity is a skill that has to be developed and maintained; you *become* objective by practicing objectivity. Describing what you see strengthens your ability to be objective as you scrutinize art in a detached, unbiased and non-judgmental way.

You need only a basic understanding of the artist's formal language, methods and materials to describe art. You need a vocabulary of appropriate, neutral terms. The usefulness of description is apparent in actual student responses to Jackson Pollock's *Convergence* and Piet Mondrian's *Composition with Blue, Red and Yellow*, before and after taking care of the prerequisites for objective looking.

JACKSON POLLOCK, Convergence (number 10, 1952), *1952.*
Abright-Knox Art Gallery, Buffalo. Gift of Seymour H. Knox, 1956.

Before: This painting is a mess! It's just paint thrown around, like the artist was mad at somebody. I don't know why this is art.

After: Pollock's *Convergence* is a large-scale non-objective oil painting. It has a horizontal format that is filled with lines and textures of overlapping threads of paint. It has intersecting marks, big gestures, and primary colors plus black and white. It is very active, full of motion, spontaneous, loud, intense, emotional.

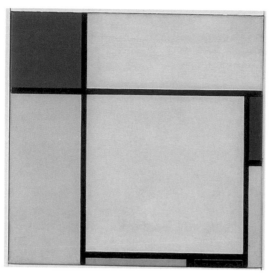

PIET MONDRIAN, Composition with Red, Blue, Yellow, and Black
Solomon R. Guggenheim Museum, New York.

Before: This looks like a package for perfume. Simple shapes that are like tiles, or children's blocks. Just a bunch of squares. This doesn't mean anything to me.

After: Mondrian's small non-objective oil painting, *Composition with Red, Blue, Yellow, and Black* contains geometric shapes (squares and rectangles) banded with black lines on a white ground. A white square dominates the picture plane with small red, yellow, blue and black shapes on the edges for emphasis and balance. He uses a primary triad for his color scheme. The lines are all straight horizontals and verticals, like a structure that is carefully built. There is no sense of movement. Stable. Static. The lines and shapes are almost identical with just small variations. Simple. Basic.

CHAPTER FOUR

GLOSSARY

Art is a language of visual signs. Its vocabulary consists of line, shape, value, texture, color and space. It is with and through these formal elements that an artist gives shape to content.

A writer uses a vocabulary of verbal signs --- words --- to make meaningful prose and poetry. A musician employs the elements of sound --- tones, chords, rests, rhythms --- to compose music. The visual artist manipulates the visual vocabulary --- the formal elements --- to make art.

> *Vocabularies are crossing circles and loops. We are defined by*
> *the lines we choose to cross or to be confined by.*
>
> (A. S. Byatt, *Possession*)

Artists understand the elements of art by making art: they learn about color by painting, about line and value by drawing, about texture and space by creating sculptural forms. In studios throughout American academia, potential artists spend semesters investigating these formal elements in design and composition courses. Every Art Appreciation textbook sets aside several chapters to dissect and analyze line, shape, value, texture, color and space, and to explore their relationships in compositions.

Here is my quandary. How basic does this need to be? What information do people really need?

Not too long ago ten college 'girlfriends' --- envision faded debutantes --- met in New Orleans to celebrate our 25th year since graduation. As we walked the campus paths under the great southern oaks, we talked leisurely and deeply about the things middle-aged women talk about: goals and dreams met and abandoned, changes, successes and disappointments, *life*.

I was the sole artist in the group --- there was a writer, a physician and a director of Off-Broadway shows --- and as we detoured through the old art building, I reminisced about art school. I don't recall the conversation, but I mentioned the paintings of Piet Mondrian. One of these friends, a woman of brilliance and accomplishment, broke in to admit, "I'm sorry, but I just don't *get* Mondrian." The group looked at me with expectant expressions. Here I was, faced with women who were well-educated, well-traveled, well-read, and they were asking me to give them some clue to Mondrian's importance. Did I dare ask the necessary question "do you know the significance of red, yellow and blue?" to such intelligent people? How else to begin talking about Mondrian? So I summoned my nerve and asked; again I got the tilted heads and questioning looks that answered, "Red, blue, yellow? Nope, not a clue."

I think that, given enough time and prompting, most folks can figure out the basic language of visual art. But if you aren't actively engaged with the visual arts on a day to day basis, it's not always easy to come up with the right term. (If a mathematician were to talk to me about *pi*, factors and integers, no matter how elementary these terms are to math, no matter how smart I think I am, I'd be lost.) The thing that justifies talking about art's vocabulary at a level that may be unnecessarily basic is that it applies to our daily lives.

We are all subjected to advertisements and visual signs whose goal is to influence our actions and habits. Since we are the targets of so much visual information, it can't hurt for us to be more aware of the visual elements and their inherent power. Like students who take design classes to analyze the elements of art, but without the advantages of hands-on experiences, let's review the basic vocabulary.

Line...

Definitions *per se* leave me cold, except for this one: A *line* is the path of a moving point! What a wonderful way to define something we 'know' without being aware of it. We also use the term line to describe the edges or *contours* of objects as they meet or overlap.

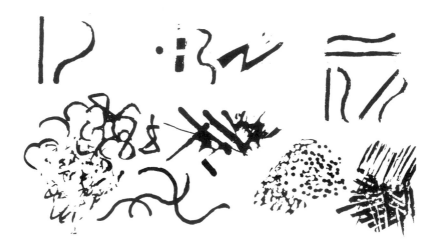

Any *actual line*, a *drawn line*, can be described in four ways: it is one of two types --- *straight* or *curved*; it has measure --- *length, width, weight*; it has direction --- either *horizontal, vertical* or *diagonal* --- and it has character --- slow, tentative, aggressive, expressive, festive, delicate, etc.

Artists group lines together --- by *stippling, hatching* or *cross-hatching* --- to create areas of gray tones, or to shade or model a representational object.

Shape...

A shape falls into one of two categories --- *geometric* and *organic* --- and is called *a mass* when it is three-dimensional. On a flat surface, the *picture plane*, we refer to the subject matter as *positive shapes* or *figure* while the 'empty' areas around and between the figure are called *negative shapes, negative space* or *ground*. A composition is the sum-total of the figure plus ground, just as music is the sum of sounds and the silences between the sounds.

Any two shapes can relate to each other in a number of ways: they can be described as *detached, touching, united, overlapping, penetrating, intersecting* or *subtracting* from each other. Some of these relationships --- overlapping and penetration --- imply that the shapes exist in actual space, and artists use them to create the illusion of depth on a flat surface.

Space...

The use of *linear perspective*, with shapes getting smaller and parallel lines appearing to converge at a *vanishing point* on the horizon line, creates a sense of depth; *atmospheric perspective* emphasizes deep space with shapes appearing to get lighter, bluer and less detailed.

One reason paintings by children and naive painters are so charming is that every detail, from foreground to far distance, is vividly described in bright colors; delightful, but *not* the way we see the world.

Value...

Light reveals objects in the visual world, and *value* is the formal element that deals with contrast between light and dark. *Mid-tone gray* lies at the visual mid-point between black and white, between *low values* and *high values*. At mid-tone gray, the optic nerve comes to rest. Some compositions are predominantly dark, in a *low key* or *low register*, just like music played below middle C; light compositions are described as having *high values*, a *high register*, a *high key*. And strong contrast between highlight and deep shadow, with few transitions between light and dark, is called *chiaroscuro*; literally light/dark.

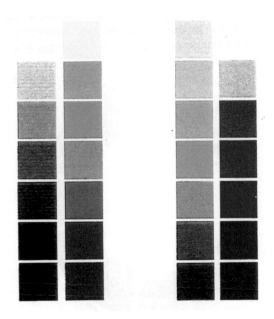

Color...

Color has value, too. Yellow has the highest value, is the lightest, and violet is the lowest or darkest. To raise the value of any color, add white, and the result is called a *tint*. We have names for some high-value colors: pink is a high value red, a tint of red; lavender is a tint of violet. Adding black to any hue lowers its value, darkens it, and creates a *shade*. (Black can also alter the appearance of colors such as yellow and orange: black plus yellow produces a wonderful 'baby-diaper green' rather than a 'dark yellow'; try it.) Adding both black and white to any color --- mid-tone gray, light gray, dark gray in varying amounts --- creates *tones*.

Colors also have *intensity*, brightness, strength, chroma; when squeezed out of a tube, the primary colors and their resulting mixtures are full strength. There is nothing you can add to a pure color to increase its intensity (Doesn't that makes sense? There is nothing you can add to pure gold to make it purer; any addition will decrease its strength and purity). The best way to decrease the intensity of a color, to dull it without altering its original hue, is to add a little of its *complement*. To dull the color yellow, add a touch of violet. Any pair of complements mixed together will eventually cancel each other out, creating a brownish, grayish non-color, a *neutral*. On a color wheel, any complementary hues produce a neutral which lies in the 'dead center'; no longer blue, no longer orange, its color has been killed, neutralized. (This is common sense, too: we know that in chemistry, acid and alkaline eventually *neutralize* each other. And on a more mundane level, if we want to take a hot bath, we fill the tub with water; if it's too hot, we add and mix in small amounts of cold to reduce the strength of the heat. Eventually, enough cold water added to the hot bath results in a tepid temperature that is neither hot nor cold.)

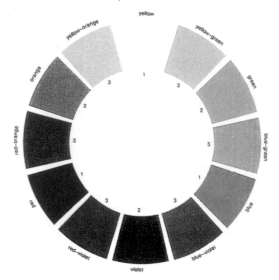

With the three *primary colors* --- red, yellow and blue --- artists mix all other hues: *secondary* and *intermediate* (aka *tertiary)* hues. From five tubes of paint (red, yellow, blue, black and white) all hues, tints, tones, shades, dull colors and neutrals can be created. Painters go into the studio with all these colors available to them, just like the chemist in the laboratory with his hundred-plus elements. Rather than using all of the possible colors, artists often limit their palettes to color schemes that can be easily identified: *monochromatic*, having a single hue; *analogous*, using related hues; *complementary*, with opposite colors; and a *triad*, with three hues that are equidistant on the color wheel.

Texture...

Some works of art have *actual texture*, surface qualities that we could experience by touching the painting or sculpture (if the museum guard would allow it). Many sculptural materials possess actual texture, and painters sometimes use a heavy application of paint called *impasto*. Other compositions include textured surfaces glued in: *collage*. Artists also create *simulated textures* with imitative drawing or painting on a smooth surface, or by printing or rubbing from actual textures. *Invented textures* create areas of visual interest and complexity through the artist's original patterns of marks.

Most of this information is familiar to us all, and we *know* it in some unconscious way. We act out the directions of line in our daily routines. When we're dressed up for formal occasions, we stand up straight, vertical, proud and dignified; doing aerobics, *moving*, we're all diagonal arms and legs; and at rest, passive and calm, we stretch out into a flat horizontal line. We deal with color theory every time we get dressed or choose a sofa pillow to add pizazz to a room. We know, on some level, that related colors create harmony and that contrast adds energy to a wardrobe or decor and grabs people's attention.

The terminology itself provides clues to its meaning: complementary colors *complete* each other: if red, yellow and blue are the equal parents of all color, then red *lacks* blue and yellow; red is *completed*, complemented by blue + yellow= green. (Trick question: what is a *compliment* of red? Answer: "You are the prettiest red I've ever seen." And the *complement* of red is green.)

The artist takes this vocabulary and, like a musician using the language of sound, composes the elements of art into arrangements that we describe as *balanced, regular, open, closed, symmetrical, radial, linear, asymmetrical.*

An artist enters the studio with an idea and sets out to give form to it. She picks and chooses from the myriad of formal possibilities, selecting those elements that serve the intention of the work. Her goal is to create a meaningful 'whole,' a unity of harmony --- through repetition, similarity, dominance and rhythm --- and variety --- with contrast and elaboration. In art as in life, too much repetition and sameness creates harmony, but the result may be predictable and boring, holding no surprises. In art as in life, too much variety can yield chaos and incoherence, conflict and war.

The artist sets out with a goal: the expression of an idea, the revelation of the work's content. She makes thousands of choices: conscious ones --- what subject matter is appropriate; what point of view; what scale; what medium; what stylistic approach; what colors, lines and shapes to use; what organization of parts --- and intuitive ones, all in service to the underlying content. Accidents happen, the unexpected occurs, and the artwork may change and take off in new and surprising directions, but very little of the process is arbitrary.

The more human beings proceed by plan, the more effectively
they may hit by accident.   (Freiderich Durrenmatt)

CHAPTER FIVE

THE LIMITATIONS OF REPRODUCTIONS

Finally, we are ready to look at art, to describe it and respond to it, and we have to admit we really aren't looking at art at all --- not at actual paintings or sculptures --- but rather at photographs of the art. In the twentieth century much of our knowledge of anything and everything comes from photographic reproductions; certainly, most of what we know about art comes from reproduced images.

Make no mistake, I appreciate having books filled with pictures of paintings and sculptures. Convenient and affordable, they are like portable museums. But the photographed images are not the same as the art; they are incomplete and, in many cases, misleading.

Some of the deficiencies are obvious. A picture of a sculpture, for example, gives us a single point of view from the fixed position of the camera. In order to fully experience a sculptural form, we must engage with it in the world of three dimensions, in space. We walk around it and view it from every possible vantage point; we participate with the sculpture, like two figures in a dance.

Reproductions of paintings, too, can be limited and untrue. A reproduction lacks subtleties. It can't reveal the texture of paint, its thickness and thinness, or the brush-work; it eliminates gestures, evidence of erasures and changes; it homogenizes the surface. Often these details don't matter, but many times they are significant and sometimes they can be crucial.

Reproduction is a simulation and, by definition, false. So while appreciating the access to the world of art that photography gives us, we need to recognize the limitations of reproductions. Simply put, the experience of viewing a photograph is not the same as viewing the work of art it represents.

Photographs of certain works put us, as viewers, in an incorrect relationship to the work. In art books, on computer screens and in lecture halls where images are projected, the size of the art is determined by the page and the screen; scale is equalized and untrue. The actual scale of the art can be critical to a correct 'reading' of it. So, when looking at any reproduction in a book or on a screen, before we do anything else, we need to note the dimensions of the art so we can mentally put ourselves in proper relationship to it. This is one of those things that, difficult at best, is important to at least acknowledge and try.

Reproductions of art can give us a false sense of scale.

Jackson Pollock, *Convergence*, 1952. Albright-Knox Art Gallery, Buffalo, New York. Gift of Seymour H. Knox, 1956.

Salvador Dali, *The Persistence of Memory*, 1931. The Museum of Modern Art, New York. Given anonymously. Photograph Copyright © 2000 The Museum of Modern Art, New York.

In a museum, we relate to paintings differently than we do looking at a book.

So when we see reproductions in a book or projected on a screen, we need to imagine ourselves in proper relationship to the art's actual size.

In a museum or gallery, I wouldn't be able to get far enough away from Jackson Pollock's monumental painting to see it the way it is shown in a book. On the page the painting is illustrated in a few concise inches, and I see the composition in its entirety. In relation to the small photograph, I am big and powerful; I dominate the image and contain the painting in a single glance. In reality, the canvas looms over my head and stretches beyond view from side to side. Standing before it, I can't see its borders, and it appears to extend forever. It overwhelms me with its powerful size; it consumes me.

Seeing a reproduction, I might mistake Pollock's painted marks as quick scribbles made by a circle of the artist's wrist, when in fact the arcs and loops of pigment are enormous gestures of arm and body, more like the sweep of a cast fishing line, a conductor's baton, a cowboy's rope... you get the idea. Scale, when it is so much larger than the body, can be important.

Small scale is worth noting, too.

The first time I saw Salvador Dali's *The Persistence of Memory*, I remember being stunned by its diminutive size, slightly larger than this book. All my life I had seen the painting reproduced in every sort of way --- on posters and calendars, even in an episode of television's *Star Trek* --- but never correctly; it was almost always reproduced larger than its actual scale.

Once I recovered from the shock of its smallness, I reconsidered the painting in relationship to its scale and made a valuable discovery: this is a private and intimate work, available to only one viewer at a time. Dali and the early Surrealists, as they thought, wrote and painted over seventy years ago, used dream imagery to explore the realm of the unconscious mind. Rather than being a disappointment, the minute scale of the painting --- about the size of my head --- became a meaningful key to a full appreciation of the work.

Now when I visit the Museum of Modern Art and see Dali's painting face to face, I like to play a little game. If no one is watching, I stand in front of the tiny canvas, so close that the imagery 'fills my head.' I think about reality, about what I know, about how I perceive through my senses: that what I know --- *reality* --- is in my head. I stand before *The Persistence of Memory* and blink my eyes over and over: closed; open; closed; open; dream; reality; subconscious; conscious.

> *It is our eyelids that separate them, but we cannot know which is inside and which outside.*   (Italo Calvino, *Invisible Cities*)

Art and Eye, coda...

Most of the information we need in order to make a connection with the artist's intention and the art's content is right in front of us, in both museums and illustrations. Museum labels and books' legends fill in some blanks --- the scale, materials and title. The date and locale of the work place it in context (a subject important enough to fill this book's second half). How simple it would be if art demanded nothing more than open minds and objective eyes, but there are times when additional questions need answering.

How does this art fit in with the artist's other work? Is its importance in its similarity or in its contrast to other work by the artist? Can the content be found in the consistency of the artist's *oeuvre* (consider Mondrian's lifelong obsession with the primary colored grid) or in the diverse totality of the artist's lifework (Picasso's art has been catalogued under 82 different styles!).

What about the artist's gender, race, or sexual orientation? More often than not this data is irrelevant, but there are times when knowing personal information about the artist will help you respond to a work appropriately. Art can be *about* sexism rather than sexist (Cindy Sherman's posed self-portraits in which she assumes history's stereotypes of 'woman pictured,' for example); *about* racial issues rather than racist (Robert Colescott's ironic paintings are important works of social criticism *because* he is African American); *about* issues of sexuality rather than homophobic or pornographic, *about* issues of faith rather than being sacrilegeous (Andres Serrano's photographs of religious articles with various humanizing and aestheticising body fluids, and the public, politicized misrepresentation of his work, illustrate this lesson).

There is some danger in applying personal information to an artist's work. Jackson Pollock's importance is *in spite of* his alcoholism, not because of it. Vincent Van Gogh's aggressive and intense symbolic paintings were *intentional* exaggerations; he was a great painter *in spite of* his mental illness, not as a result of it. And while Van Gogh's countless depictions of flowers don't seem to require tedious gender-based interpretations, Georgia O'Keefe's floral paintings are too often ascribed to 'the feminine,' while the same sort of analysis is absent from her numerous images of rigid, vertical city buildings. Artists' personalities and life experiences are certainly tied to the art they produce, but some information can mislead you.

CHAPTER SIX

ART AND I

When you look at a work of art and respond to it with a vocabulary of non-judgmental terms, you are buying time: time to practice objectivity and to consider the choices made by the artist in service to the work's content, its function, its meaning. There are other ways to grasp the essence of the work, ways that are more personal, subjective, interpretive, even fun!

Consider what was required of the artist to create any particular work. What specific preparations, tools, physical and mental attitudes, body language would be necessary to make it?

Identify with the process: if you were making a work like this, how would you *feel*? Would you be quiet and contemplative? Slow and methodical? Deliberate? Energetic? Spontaneous? Quiet? Aggressive? Meditative? Gentle?

Sound it out (in your imagination or in the privacy of your room, *not* in a museum, please). If it were music, how might it sound? If it were a sound in nature, what might it be? If it were a word or noise, would it be a whisper? A tortured groan? An explosion?

Let it *move* you (again, do this privately). If it were a dance, what would it be? Flowing? Staccato? A march? A yoga pose?

Consider equivalents from the world outside of art, music and dance. Think about what it *is like* rather than what it *looks like*. In other words, try to translate the artwork into analogous 'others.'

Objectivity helps us describe what the work *is*; appropriate, non-judgmental subjective responses help us think of what the work *is like*. Using both objective and subjective responses gives us insight into possible content and intention of artworks, as the following case studies demonstrate.

Jackson Pollock, *Convergence (Number 10, 1952),* Oil on canvas, 93½ x 156 in.
Albright-Knox Art Gallery, Buffalo, New York. Gift of Seymour H. Knox, 1956.

Jackson Pollock's *Convergence*, described objectively, *is* a two-dimensional, non-objective oil painting; it is monumental in scale, with a horizontal format. It has an overall composition with no focal point, composed of complex, varied, overlapping lines and textures. It contains primary colors, black and white; the pigment creates skeins of color and texture. It is energetic, emotional, powerful, bold, free, spontaneous. It is made of grand gestures, with no beginning and no end.

Making this painting, the artist probably had no fixed notion of its outcome... he just let it happen, editing during the process... no self-consciousness... once he starts a passage or color, he can't stop... automatic responses, free from conscious decision-making... internal, intuitive... there is the potential for error and disaster... abandon with just enough control... confident... physical... a performance... strong... potent... virile. RELEASE.

It *is like* a carnival... Mardi Gras... a celebration... midway at the fair... a ticker-tape parade... noisy... a babble of sound... a cocktail party... improvisational jazz...Beethoven's *Eroica*... a stampede... a bucking bronco... a free-style high-dive... the *William Tell Overture*... the Blue Angels... trapeze acrobatics without a net... a tribal sand painting... a ritual of dance and sound... *Bring in da Noise*... an ant farm in high gear... a thunderstorm... energy... Robin Williams after lots of coffee... electricity... the movement of the cosmos... conducting Rossini's *Barber of Seville*... riding a Harley, wide open... a whirling dervish... speaking in tongues... filled with the spirit... ecstasy. Oh man, just let yourself *GO*...

Piet Mondrian, *Composition with Red, Blue, Yellow, and Black, 1929.* Oil on canvas.
17 3/4 x 17 7/8". Solomon R. Guggenheim Museum, New York.
Photograph by David Heald ©The Solomon R. Guggenheim Foundation, New York.

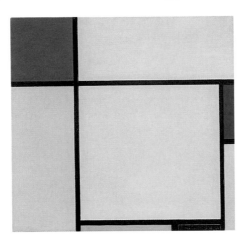

Piet Mondrian's *Composition with Red, Blue, Yellow, and Black* is a small non-objective oil painting composed of eight shapes, squares and rectangles which are similar while being varied in size and proportion. White is dominant, with a central white square. He uses primary colors along the edges (they create energy!) in tiny shapes that are separated/held together by a grid of black horizontal and vertical lines on a white ground. The painting is structured and contemplated, with corrections that suggest thoughtful changes and revisions. It is mechanical, elemental and reductive. Stable, balanced, regular and complete. It is impersonal, unemotional, careful, methodical, analytical. Slow. Every action (each shape, each line) determines every other reaction. It is brought into completion as it goes, not preconceived, but deliberately brought into being.

Sitting at a table, standing before a drawing board, he confronts the empty picture plane. Where to begin? There are no guidelines, no rules, no single 'right' way. Would he have used a straight-edge? A ruler? Masking tape? I don't think so... Concentrate, consider, edit, consider, ponder, consider, decide.

It is like a drill team... a color guard... *The March of the Marionettes*... Seals and Crofts... Willie Nelson's voice... a barbershop quartet... a fugue... water brought to the boiling point... a carpenter's level... a tight-rope walker... karate... t'ai chi... a magnet... a chiropractic adjustment... haiku... a centrifuge... a chess game... a balanced equation.

Henri Matisse, *Large Composition with Masks*, 1953. Collage, paper on canvas.
11'7¼" x 32'8⅛". National Gallery of Art, Washington, D.C.
Ailsa Mellon Bruce Fund, 1973.

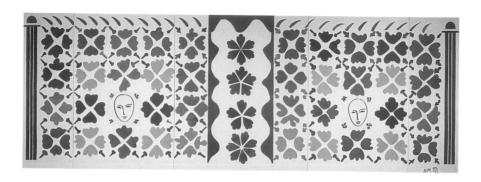

Matisse's *Large Composition with Masks* is a monumental, abstract, horizontal composition of cut paper with orderly rows of detached shapes on a white ground, creating a flat decorative pattern. It is symmetrical and linear, with occasional surprises of color and slight variations of shapes. Sharp edges. Defined. Punctuated.

The design was probably pre-determined, planned in advance. The artist could be thinking about dinner or the stock market while assembling the work. The creativity was in making the preliminary designs, then in arranging, changing, editing, etc.

Pow, pow, pow... a cheer... hopscotch... a fiesta... fireworks... popcorn... step-aerobics... hip-hop... flamenco... dancing a polka... drumbeats... percussion... syncopation... the Gypsy Kings... *Shall We Dance?* 1,2,3... Bobby McFerrin... disco... dealing a hand of cards... boxers sparring... tap... rap... FUN!

Agnes Martin, *Night Sea* (1963). Oil and gold leaf on canvas. 6' x 6'.
Private collection, courtesy Pace Wildenstein Gallery, New York.

Agnes Martin's *Night Sea* is a non-objective painting in oil and gold leaf. It has a square format, composed of regular rows of geometric shapes (rectangles), with slight variations, a cool blue, and a grid of horizontal and vertical lines. A delicate web of gold... calm... subtle... passive... quiet... elegant. Simple. Eternal.

A reproduction doesn't reveal whether the ground is gold with blue shapes applied to it or whether the lines are drawn on a blue ground. Either way, the process would be slow, repetitious, concentrated, with intense focus. Precise, careful. Hypnotic. Reverent.

I am moved to stillness... revery... quiet... like a spider's web... a pendulum... a hypnotist's bob... perpetual motion... a metronome... a clock... a steady heartbeat... a pulse... a funeral cortege... Philip Glass... John Cage... Tibetan monks chanting... a mantra... meditation: breathe in, breathe out... the rhythms of nature: sunrise, sunset... ebb and flow... the drip of a melting icicle... running a marathon...tip-toe, tip-toe... a spinning wheel... a trance... a prayer...ohmmm... shhhh...

A FINAL THOUGHT

We look at art and we want to Get It. We want to know what it's 'about,' its point, what it means. But sometimes searching for a literal and specific meaning or reading too much into any work of art may in fact be counter-productive.

There was a little scene in the movie *Bodies, Rest and Motion* that stuck in my mind: the hero confronted a Native American man during a windstorm in the Arizona desert and asked what the wind might mean.

The Indian looked confused. "......Hunh???"

"The wind," insisted the young man. "What does it mean?" He was determined for the weather to signify something important, to contain some secret or mystery, and he kept suggesting possibilities: ancestral spirits, perhaps? a tribal change? an angry Earth?

He finally got an answer. "......The wind? ......It's just the wind."

Art is sometimes like the wind. It may not 'mean' in any literal sense, but like the atmosphere preceding a storm, it puts us into a frame of mind for pondering the timeless questions of existence and meaning.

PART TWO

HISTORY LESSONS

CHAPTER SEVEN

THE CANON

When I first taught Art Appreciation at a university in the American Midwest, I prefaced the art history lectures with the statement: *We are all Greeks,* which seemed to make sense. Now, teaching on the Mexican-American border, that introduction seems ludicrous. And with time being so precious, I find myself considering whether a survey of Western Civilization is an absolute necessity. Every semester I decide that it is.

First, we all need to acknowledge that the story of Western Civilization still shapes our lives in very fundamental ways: our language and religions, architecture and attitudes toward beauty, mythological references, our governmental structure, all are traceable in a direct line back to the ancient Greeks and, before them, to the kingdoms of Egypt. Many of my students live south of the Rio Grande, and while they know the names and facts of Mexico's rich history, the information I present in the brief survey of Western Civilization may be new to them. And finally, while my young students have a good knowledge of computer skills, many of them have not been introduced to what seemed basic to those of us who were educated before the advent of the digital age. Again, I decide to take little for granted and to present or review information of a general and basic nature; again, it can't hurt.

I punctuate the art history unit with a refrain: *This is not an art history class, and I am not an art historian.* There are advantages to teaching the history of art from a non-scholarly position: since I only deal with these topics once a semester --- and since, at mid-life, my memory is less than perfect --- I have the thrill of re-learning the lessons and of getting re-enthused about each subject. If I were a·scholar in any one of these historical areas, I might be expected to have answers to the specific questions the students ask; instead, I get to tell them a truth I've discovered: that, if one has the time or interest, one can explore any topic and find the answers. One doesn't have to know everything about a subject to get meaning from it, and sometimes the questions, unanswered, are satisfying enough in the asking.

Even a superficial survey of Western Civilization provides valuable rewards. Our vocabulary increases, and we can connect with cultural references that might have been 'foreign' to us before; we learn a few words of Greek, Italian, and French; we discover meaning in the origin of labels --- Middle Ages, Renaissance, Gothic, Baroque ---; we recognize and identify historic influences that surround us today; we think of history in a meaningful order; and we have topics galore for future research projects: the history of calendars, gender/power differences expressed through coloration of Egyptian painting, an analysis of Egyptian sculptural iconography, the original colors of Greek sculpture and architecture, attitudes toward women in --- pick one: ancient Greece, the Medieval Period, the Renaissance ---, the history of institutionalized Christianity, the history of the New Testament, Neo-Platonism, changing attitudes toward masculinity in the *David* sculpture of Donatello compared to that by Michelangelo, the list goes on and on.

In a perfect world we would all know a lot about many things. We would recognize the living tradition of Western Civilization and bring our knowledge of that tradition to our understanding of art. Ideally we would all take art history courses and, as long as I am free to fantasize, we would retain the information and dates presented in those classes. In the mean time and in the real world, there are many useful lessons that we can learn from a superficial glance at art history, lessons that can help us see art in a more meaningful way.

Even the scantiest overview of Western art history provides us the chance to review some facts, to get a long-distance perspective, and to view the tradition of Western Civilization as a long, evolving story whose influence still shapes our lives.

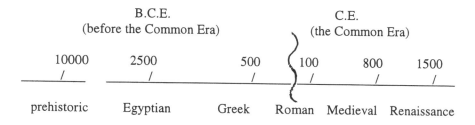

The story of Western art teaches us, over and over, a basic lesson: art embodies the culture that produces it. The art of a particular society or period expresses the goals, values, ideas and ideals emphasized by that culture or period. If you know something about any given culture, you automatically know something about its art, and vice-versa.

This fundamental lesson becomes evident right from the start if you compare the figurative sculptures of ancient Egypt and Classical Greece. Situated in the deserts of northern Africa, the Egyptian kingdoms were insulated from invasion and isolated from visitors; every aspect of life was repetitious and linear, from the north-south line of the Nile River, to the east-west movement of the sun across the desert sky. The art of Egypt, protected from outside influences, remained relatively unchanged for nearly 3000 years and is characterized by linear rhythms and repetitions.

The sculpture of ancient Greece made a dramatic departure from the rigid poses of their Egyptian sources, a change you can easily grasp if you mimic the forms: stand like a carved Egyptian figure with your torso straight, arms close to the body, fists closed and one leg stiffly presented to the front with a locked knee; then shift your weight to one leg, freeing the other to act as a counterbalance in the manner of Classical Greek sculpture. Can't you *feel* the different emphasis? Classical Greek art expressed the culture's goal, the individual search for 'the Divine Center.' By assuming a relaxed stance with your balance on one foot --- *contrapposto* --- you embody through your body what the art expresses: balance, equilibrium, and the freedom to move into any active pose while remaining in perfect balance. (Keep in mind: the sculpture and architecture of ancient civilizations were originally painted with vivid colors; our idea of them as bare stone is misleading.)

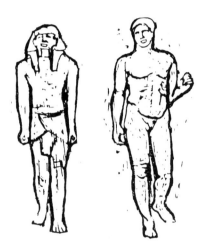

The usefulness of 'body work' came to me by accident on one of those non-verbal days that are the bane of lecturers. I was scheduled to talk about the Medieval Period, that millennium of relative stasis in art and intellectual activity between the Greco-Roman era and its rebirth a thousand years later in the Italian Renaissance, two peaks of artistic achievement. Looking at the flat line of the Medieval Period, I noted that around 1000 C.E. some significant things happened. Two styles of church architecture appeared, suggesting major changes. Instead of describing these styles in words or notes on the board --- I was tired and tongue-tied --- I acted them out. First I 'became' a Romanesque church: head lowered, eyes closed, I stood heavily planted with my arms and weight directed downward. Then, imitating the Gothic, with arms sweeping up, up, up, I assumed the pointed arch form; I took a deep inhaling breath and opened my eyes like windows letting in light.

Romanesque and Gothic architecture signify the shift from the Medieval world view --- fatalistic, mysterious, dark, earth-bound --- to the Renaissance spirit of Humanistic enquiry. Reaching up, I aspired toward God; breathing in, I was inspired; and eyes open, light flooded in and I was illuminated.

If art embodies the culture --- and it does --- then we can 'embody' the art through physical acting-out and arrive, full circle, at its significance and meaningfulness.

CHAPTER EIGHT

SHORT CUTS

Ebb and flow...

Art styles don't appear fully formed; they evolve and devolve in a pattern that can be described with a swelling curve, an ebb and flow. Although this model, like any over-simplification and generalization, is subject to many exceptions and contradictions, it can be frequently applied to a general understanding of art history.

Typically, the early phase, the *archaic*, is developmental, with forms that are often crude, tentative and imperfect. The height of the culture is frequently called its *Classic* phase, and it is at this peak that the forms of art are fully established and perfected. Since this phase can't be sustained indefinitely, *post-Classic* art tends to degenerate into elaboration, exaggerated movement and ornamental excess.

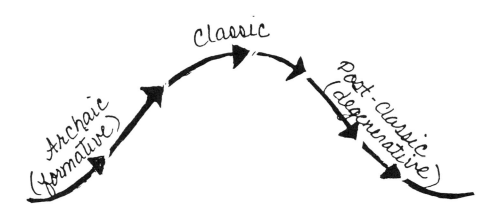

Early Greek sculptors took their artistic cues from their teachers in ancient Egypt, and archaic Greek sculpture looks Egyptian in its pose. (Archaic Greek figures copied the iconography of their Egyptian models, with the forward foot signifying royal birth, and the fist closed around a gold cylinder connoting power. I can visualize an early Greek sculptor bringing his methods, imagery and style from Egypt and being asked *Why that position of foot? Why the fist? I don't know*, his answer might have been; *this is how all sculpture looks...*)

In one of the greatest achievements of Western art, Greek figurative sculpture evolved in only 150 years from the awkward archaic pose into idealized forms and perfected carving, with its relaxed *contrapposto* and the potential to express dynamic gestures. The Classical *kouros* and *kore* figures embodied Greece's emphasis on 'the center,' establishing an ideal through measurement and proportion, creating relationships and harmony of all parts, and the realization of the whole.

Post-classic Greek art, like that of the post-Classic Mayan civilization and the art of the post-Renaissance in Europe, gave way to increasing decoration and technical showmanship, with drama and emotionality replacing the pure, rational, unencumbered balance of 'the Classic.' The ebb and flow of styles is demonstrated two thousand years later in the rebirth of Classical art in the Italian Renaissance.

A model like 'ebb and flow' is useful only when it is useful; it is counterproductive to try to force every artwork or cultural example to fit any single model. Still, considering the ebb and flow of cultures and the art that embodies them can help us make reasonable assumptions and place artworks in a proper chronology --- walking around the cities of Europe, for example.

Students ask if this model might be applied to the present to help us see ourselves and our society in 'the now.' Perhaps. But in a world defined by rapid change and pluralism, with competing ideas occurring simultaneously, a model for contemporary times might resemble an EKG during a fibrillating event rather than a gradual, understandable and predictable curve.

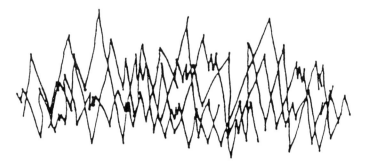

Pendulum swings...

A review of art history provides numerous examples of art's momentum as action and reaction: the rational calm of High Renaissance art, for example, was rejected by the next generation of Mannerist painters. There is a spiritual reality, they suggested, that cannot be revealed through reason alone. Similarly, at the beginning of the Modern Period, Romantic painters counteracted the Neoclassical emphasis on order and reason with a style characterized by theatrical lighting, dynamic movement, expressive color and passion. The pendulum swings.

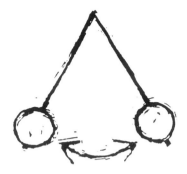

CLASSICAL	ROMANTIC
rational	emotional
measured	spontaneous
balanced	dynamic
carefully drawn	vigorously colored
intellectual	spiritual
theoretical	intuitive
universal	personal
outward-directed	inner-directed
sense	sensibility

Compare Leonardo's *Last Supper* to Tintoretto's treatment of the same subject matter nearly a century later and you can see the backlash of Baroque painting to the balanced order of the High Renaissance:

David's composition for *The Death of Socrates* illustrates Neoclassical calm in contrast to the Romantic expressiveness of Delacroix's *Liberty Leading the People*.

Head and heart...

CLASSICAL

*Art should have no higher guide
than the torch of Reason.*
                    (Jacque-Louis David)

ROMANTIC

*The heart has its reasons that
Reason cannot know.*
                    (Pascal, *Pensees*)

The Classical periods of Greece and Rome may be ancient history. The celebration of renewed classical ideals by Renaissance artists and thinkers has long since subsided. And the 19th-century battle between Neoclassical painters and Romantic artists is to us passé. But the model of head and heart is still a useful one. We can recognize these two traditions in the works of many Modernist and contemporary artists: Piet Mondrian's work lies clearly on the side of classical art, while Jackson Pollock's paintings could be appropriately described as being romantic.

The terms *classical* and *romantic*, detached from their origins, are not judgmental ones. There has been and continues to be great art and lesser art that predominantly serves the mind, greater and lesser art that expresses heart and soul. The artist working in the classical tradition seeks 'the point' by abnegating self and exploring the world of theory, while an artist aligned with the romantic tradition turns inward toward truth. Neither way is in itself superior or inferior to the other; they are two different paths that aim toward the same ultimate destination.

Clues...

The innovations made by artists over time provide useful clues for making educated guesses about when and where a work of art or architecture may have originated. Since linear perspective wasn't developed until 1450, early and awkward examples of perspective in painting lead us to deduce that the painting may have been made in the early Renaissance. Here are a few technical and artistic achievements that provide us with helpful hints:

> Early Greek sculpture may look a lot like Egyptian figures, but the Greeks penetrated the negative spaces between legs, arms and torso. Fully articulated movement in carved sculpture is probably Greek or later.

> Imperial Romans rediscovered and deserve credit for utilizing the true, round arch and its resulting forms: the tunnel vault and the dome. So architecture using these forms (which are still in use today) could not have been made prior to the Roman empire.

> Roman artists absorbed and copied the idealized forms of ancient Greece, but they added true realism to their portraiture; people are portrayed as they appear --- aging, worried, tired, plain, the *real* rather than the *ideal*.

> Oil paint and linear perspective were developed during the early Renaissance. Add those innovations to the Humanistic fascination with individual personality and you can see how painting's greater realism occurred.

I'm always amazed how far a little knowledge and common sense can go...

CHAPTER NINE

MAKING PROGRESS

After taking a telescopic view of 3000 years of Western art, we owe ourselves a more leisurely approach to the art of the Modern Period. After all, we are active participants in the ongoing modern tradition, and the lessons and contributions of Modernism influence just about everything we see, think and do. A model for the Modern Period might be a straight line or a series of parallel, advancing arrows, illustrating *progress*, Modernism's faith in progress and the inevitability of progress.

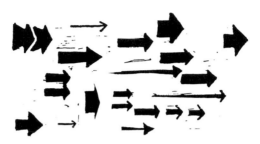

Modernist ideas and art moved forward by asking question which, once asked, never needed to be asked again:

> In 19th-century Europe, Romantic artists posed the question: why must art look to the past for inspiration? Why can't art deal with contemporary subject matter?

> 19th-century Realists asked: why must art inspire, moralize, or sit in judgment? Why can't art present 'the real' as it is, without preferring beauty to ugliness or virtue to vice?

> Impressionists asked important questions about perception and the nature of reality-as-seen. Cubists considered the dimension of time; the Fauves questioned the descriptive and symbolic function of color and set color free; the German Expressionists furthered the idea through the distortion of all form to directly express emotion, and created the first non-objective painting.

> Dada asked: does art lie in the production of forms? Can meaning, suggested by Modernist formalism, exist in an apparently senseless world? And what about the reality of the unconscious mind? queried the Surrealists. What about accidents and chance?

> American painters of the New York School, labeled Abstract Expressionists, pondered the possibility of individualism in the modern state. And Pop Art asked: is packaging the product?

The styles and content of Modernist art didn't originate unassisted; they parallel ideas, philosophies and discoveries being investigated throughout the culture:

CONTEXT	→	STYLE
photography		Impressionism
speed, flight e=mc2		Cubism
WWI		dada
current events		German Expressionism
psychoanalysis		Surrealism
current events		Abstraction
Cold War		Abstract Expressionism
the media consumerism		Pop Art

The technical innovations and contributions of Modernism evolved along with its ideas. Like the questions posed by Modern art, new media and attitudes became a permanent part of the artistic vocabulary.

STYLE	→	CONTRIBUTION
Impressionism		Broken color, visible brushstroke
Fauvism		Arbitrary color
Cubism		Simultaneity, collage
Expressionism		Elimination of subject matter
Dada		Ready-mades
Surrealism		Automatism

CHAPTER TEN

TO SEE

Impressionist art, even in paintings created 100 years after the style's heyday, is easy to recognize by its stylistic characteristics: the independent brushstroke and partially mixed, 'optical' color.

Imagine that the time is 1875 and the place is Paris, France. Imagine that I am a painter and I decide to go outside and paint directly from nature. Today this would hardly seem like a radical idea, but a century ago it was an unheard-of break with the tradition of painting established in the Renaissance. In 1875 my teachers and fellow artists would be constructing their subject matter in the studio, working from posed models according to long-held views of academic composition and craftsmanship.

There would be many reasons compelling me to paint in this new way at the end of the 19th century: pigment is being manufactured in tubes which make paint portable; the city is being transformed from its Medieval past to a wonderland of boulevards and gardens; the literature and philosophy of the period celebrate nature; and the growing middle-class is enjoying its leisure time in the parks and sidewalk cafes. It is *la belle epoque*, and out-of-doors is where it's happening in the Paris of 1875.

Let's say that I have been contemplating how any of us knows what we know (a question many artists consider, whatever their epoch). Let's say that I have been thinking that we either trust someone else's description of a thing, or we know that thing by seeing it, witnessing it, picturing it with our own eyes. I want to portray on my canvas exactly what I know through my eyes, what I see as I see it. I refuse to depend on memory, since memory is unreliable, and I avoid using my imagination which is equally faulty.

Instead, I look at whatever is out there --- the subject matter is beside the point; let's say it is a row of trees --- and I translate it into paint, without sentiment or interpretation. All I want to do is to see, honestly and completely.

My painting begins with a quick overall sketch to establish the scale and to organize the shapes on the picture plane. As I look at the patterns of dark and light and the relationships of colors, I notice that just as I start to paint, those very colors change, the highlights shift, and the shadows move. If a breeze blows, I realize that I see leaves as a mere impression of shimmering light and color rather than as individual shapes.

I must rethink my entire method of painting. There isn't enough time for compositional organization, underpainting, or careful color mixing, all the things considered basic to painting. To capture any particular 'reality,' which changes as the sun moves overhead or the wind blows, I have to paint very quickly. In order to depict what I see and to be true to the immediacy of seeing it, I must capture the sensory impression of forms, expressed through light and color, as it happens.

I don't have time to thoroughly mix the various hues, but I discover that colors can be combined by the viewer's eye. And I can't carefully blend the brushstrokes and eliminate the evidence of my hand, as I might in the studio, but I recognize the energy that the visible strokes of pigment and texture give to the surface.

During the 1870s in Paris, a group of artists set out to record visual reality as seen --- not as imagined or remembered --- and took their paints out of doors into the world of nature, light and atmosphere. Their inquiry into the act of seeing resulted in Impressionism, a style that is easily identified by its characteristics: broken color --- partially mixed pigment which is optically blended by the viewer --- and the independent brushstroke.

Of course we look at art from the outside, but it may help us Get It if we think about it from the inside out. Too often we consider art to be nothing more than style, instead of seeing style as the logical, visible outcome of the painter's intention and process. True, the next generation of Impressionists did pattern their use of color and brushwork after the earlier painters, using style as a starting point. And they made some wonderful paintings along the way. But the importance of Impressionism is in its intention rather than its outcome, its style.

There are people who still paint in the manner of the early Impressionists. The process may be instructive and satisfying to the painter, and the results may be nice to look at, but a century after its origin, Impressionism as a style is no more important to art than dropping apples from high places is important to physics. Impressionist paintings are popular and valuable, but the essential value of Impressionism lies in what it accomplished in its time. Through an intense and uncompromising visual engagement with nature, these early modern artists liberated the act of seeing, and through their work they asked questions that remain worth considering:

What is the 'real' color of any thing?

What is 'true'? And how does one know?

Is there a fixed reality? Is perception reality?

Are perception and reality relative?

By the beginning of the twentieth century, Impressionism was generally accepted and increasingly popular. Today we use reproductions of Impresssionist paintings to decorate fabrics and note cards, coffee mugs and calendars. To our eyes, this is one style that we can agree is pretty and likeable. It is hard to believe that in 1875, people saw these compositions of dissolving shapes and shimmering colors and considered them to be ugly. Gerome, the former head of the Academy of Painting and Sculpture which was the era's voice of aesthetic authority, described Impressionist paintings as "filth representing a great moral slackening."

Gerome and his peers were not mentally deficient; to the uninitiated eye of a hundred years past, Impressionism *was* ugly. Our 20th-century eyes have been conditioned since birth by photographs and film, so it is easy for us to make sense of the soft focus and disintegrating edges of Impressionist painting. But when it was first exhibited, the display of brushstrokes and unblended color was the visual equivalent of hearing an unknown language: meaningless nonsense, gibberish, noise. People of intelligence and sophistication condemned Impressionist art as "shitty painting," and "a threat to the nation."

When we see something new --- or hear it: think rap music --- we lack the means to process it. Since we can't easily fit 'the new' into any category, it can seem frightening, confusing, alienating, ugly. (Warning: this is not an equivalent equation. While 'the new' is often considered to be ugly, ugly/ new things do not always become easy to understand or increasingly valuable as Impressionist paintings have done.)

As hard as I try, I can't envision a world without photography. Like the computer in the twentieth century, the camera evolved from a large, cumbersome and expensive tool to a small, affordable and ubiquitous necessity. By 1874, when a group of painters formed the Society of Independent Artists later labeled as Impressionists --- "*mere* impressionists," they were derided ---, photographs were being produced and reproduced everywhere. What must it have been like to see those first photographic images?

The Impressionists may have been of two minds as they critiqued the shared visual reality of early photography. First, the camera enabled movement to be stilled, examined and understood. Imagine painting, from life, the fluid surface of a swimming pool: paintbrush ready, you look at the water and think *okay... ready... here goes... I've got it... I've got it...* but the surface never stops moving, the patterns shift and merge. It is hard to see the patterns of movement until we examine movement stilled.

Eadweard Muybridge's photographs of figures in stop-action stills must have been a revelation to artists when his images of human and animal locomotion were published in 1887. *Now* they could see the movement of reflections on water, of steam from train engines, of the horse race. (Pre-camera depictions of galloping horses presented their legs in impossible, invented positions; before seeing still photographs, how could one know?)

At the same time, these painters surely recognized that a still photograph is a false record of the experience of seeing, thus discovering a new truth which is the underlying tenet of Impressionism: visual reality is transitory. It --- nature, light, atmosphere, *life* --- is never still. While the photographer replaced the painter as record-keeper and documentarian, the Impressionist artists went outdoors in order to look. And they painted in order to see.

CHAPTER ELEVEN

ART AND EXPERIENCE

This Neo-Cubist collage presents numerous aspects of the coffee cup, arranged on a Modernist grid.

If a Renaissance painter were to describe a simple cup, he might place it on a table in front of an open window and construct the image on his canvas by viewing the object from a fixed vantage point, applying the laws of linear perspective and carefully rendering all visible details. Four hundred years later, an Impressionist painter might arrange the cup on a table outdoors on a sunny day and respond to the play of light and color across its surface, again from a single viewpoint. But early in the twentieth century, some artists found the Impressionist manner of seeing and painting to be inadequate to the full description of and response to a reality beyond surface appearance.

Their thinking might have gone like this: if my goal is to describe a cup and to depict it completely, I can't just look at it from one point of view. I must pick it up and examine it from all sides; I tilt it, raise it over my head, and look at the bottom. If it is full of coffee, perhaps I take a sip. As I drink from the cup, I might glance at a newspaper. I put the cup down and leave a series of circular stains on the tablecloth.

To fully know 'cup,' I have to describe its totality. It takes more than measuring it in three dimensions from a single perspective; it requires the fourth dimension --- time --- to completely experience the cup, to look at it from multiple viewpoints and to see its parts and its whole.

Pablo Picasso and George Braque, working in tandem during the first decade of the century, confronted this problem: how can an artist describe the world of experience within the single frame of a painting's surface? Their solution was Cubism. Uninterested in the Impressionists' obsession with effects of light and color as they define the surface of objects, the early Cubists set out to translate the whole of experience onto the picture plane.

Fact: we never see the world from a fixed position. The optic nerve vibrates, our eyes move, our head shifts position, and we perceive reality in bits and pieces. Walking from point A to point B, we construct a useful composite of views, our eyes functioning much like a camera lens: focusing on details, then pulling back for a long view, re-focusing, shifting our point of view and range of vision. We piece together a meaningful reality that allows us to negotiate with objects in space. To the Cubist artists, the picture plane became the arena on which they acted out the experience of seeing, recording subject matter from multiple viewpoints at once, in facets that disintegrate, accumulate and reconfigure.

It was no accident that Picasso and Braque developed this new way of seeing at the same time Albert Einstein published his theory of relativity. Concurrent to the early Cubist works, Einstein was using pure math and physics to explore the fourth dimension of time and space. The artists declared they were not influenced by any theory, and there is no reason to think that they read obscure and esoteric theories of contemporary science. But the collusion of ideas is not mere coincidence. At its highest level, art runs on a track parallel to those of pure science, mathematics, theology, philosophy, music and literature. The world of Picasso, Braque and Einstein was one of unprecedented change and increasing speed. People climbed the Eiffel Tower, flew in early airplanes and hot air balloons, and saw their world from new heights, and simple perspective in relation to the horizon line was forever altered.

The contributions of Cubist art are immeasurable. Whether contemporary artists acknowledge it or not, they have all been influenced by Cubism's innovations and techniques. Modern architecture, furniture and fashion design, typography and graphic layout, even imagery on MTV are all indebted to the Cubist revolution. As for painting, the picture plane which for four centuries had functioned as a 'window' to the visual world was forever revolutionized. By 1910, the painting surface had been transformed into a planar field on which the experience of reality, not merely its visible surface appearance, could be recorded and expressed.

CHAPTER TWELVE

ART AND MEANING

This playful variation on Marcel Duchamp's *L.H.O.O.Q.* illustrates the irreverent spirit of *dada*.

Look through any art history book that surveys the story of Western art and you will see that the transition from representational art to that of abstraction is obvious. It occurs shortly after Impressionism, and as you turn the pages of art history, you'll see that it is both a gradual change and a rapid one. At the beginning of the twentieth century, the Fauve painters declared color to be free from its descriptive and symbolic function. Taking the next step forward, German Expressionists distorted form as well as color to express emotions relevant to 'the modern condition' --- alienation, anxiety, paranoia and isolation. The Cubists disintegrated form, then reassembled it into dynamic compositional wholes. By 1910, this revolution in painting was pretty much complete.

That was when Wassily Kandinsky created the first non-objective painting, eliminating the depiction of subject matter altogether. The vocabulary of line, shape and color spoke directly to the viewer, as music does to the listener, without referring to subject matter or symbol.

The camera was recording events and reproducing scenes, while art of the Modern Period was free to express inner realities of idea and emotion. Abstraction was, and still is, a huge umbrella that encompasses all manner of forms: subject matter is distorted, simplified, elaborated, geometricized, or completely abandoned in favor of pure non-objectivity. The formal elements serve the compositional and expressive needs of the artwork. In the Modern Period, art's function changed. It began to address its own issues. It became art for Art's sake.

If you share the Modernist view of art, you accept the idea that forms have their own potential, that they are their own truth. Art has a universal power to speak to us directly, to connect us at our most human and humane levels, to be meaningful and therefore to create meaning. You believe in the power of art and the power of meaning.

If you are a sculptor, you might want to make a work of art in keeping with these beliefs: you decide it will be non-objective, with no reference to subject matter. It will be made of a simple material, white, hard, and polished so it will reflect light and cast shadows; it will have subtle convex and concave forms; it will be penetrated here and there with circular openings that create an interplay of positive and negative spaces. You give it the title *Fountain*, sign it, and take it to a gallery for public display. You are an artist, and your *Fountain* is art.

Again, let's say that, as a Modernist sculptor with the loftiest goals, you desire to make a work that contains the sum of all things in the most elemental way. Perhaps this is some expression of your idea of God. As such, it would have no beginning and no end; you decide on an open circle. You create lines that spread from the center, suggesting an eternal going out and coming in. When the circle is still, you can reach through its radiating lines; when it spins, the same form defies penetration. It is a sculpture, so you put it on a pedestal.

I have just described two works 'created' by Marcel Duchamp around 1915. Before it was a sculpture, Duchamp's *Fountain* was nothing more than a common urinal, the last thing one would expect to see in the elite and sophisticated gallery setting of early Modernist art. The second example combined a bicycle wheel inverted on a crude kitchen stool. Duchamp, a respected artist of utmost seriousness, did not craft any of the forms; they were already made, 'found objects' from the everyday world.

Please don't misunderstand these examples. Duchamp's *Wheel* was not intended to be an evocation of God, nor was the urinal selected because of its inherent formal attributes. Duchamp's art was decidedly and intentionally anti-aesthetic. I take liberties here to make a point. If an artist were to create works in the fanciful manner I have described, we would nod our heads in approval: Art.

If you think about it in this way, a urinal detached from its pipes and from its designed function meets the requirements of non-representational Modernist sculpture; no longer useful as plumbing, it functions only in a formal sense. You can't ride the bicycle wheel; it only 'works' as a sculptural form. The stool, denied its original function, becomes viable as a pedestal. In the context of an art gallery, these quotidian objects become art.

Duchamp and his cohorts from the world of art, literature and philosophy were responding to the horror and senselessness of the First World War and reacting to society's moral void. These artists and thinkers, under the intentionally meaningless moniker *dada*, despaired of 'civilization.' If, in the 3000-year tradition of Western Civilization, mankind has been unable to think its way to rational behavior, they suggested, how dare artists presume to make meaning in a warring and apparently irrational world? It was a good question then, and I think it still is.

Duchamp's 'ready-mades' --- objects produced for other purposes by craftsmen or machines --- were intended to repudiate the notion of Modern Art as a reflection of civilization and proof of humankind's moral superiority. But *dada*, a movement born out of opposition to aesthetics, manners and rational behavior, was doomed to failure. A nihilistic, in-your-face celebration of absurdity and senselessness, it kept making sense!

Another of Duchamp's ready-mades, titled *L.H.O.O.Q.*, fully expresses the spirit of *dada*. Of course, Duchamp did not create the painting of Mona Lisa or even make the copied image. The Dadaist work is a small reproduction of Leonardo Da Vinci's masterpiece, the singular artwork that embodies Western Civilization. People will wait for hours to glimpse this Renaissance painting behind bullet-proof glass, not because it is the Western world's greatest painting or even Leonardo's finest achievement, but because it has become a cultural icon through infinite reproduction.

Duchamp took a cheap postcard and cheapened it further, insulting the image with a drawn mustache and goatee. Beneath the picture he inscribed the letters *L.H.O.O.Q.* which when said aloud ---*elle a chaud au queue* (she's got a hot ass) --- label the grand dame of High Art and, by implication, art itself as a whore. In the context of the Great War, *dada*'s anti-sense made a strong statement. We're blowing each other and the world into oblivion. We're killing and dying and rotting in the trenches. Meaning? Order? Humanism? Civilization? Art?

Duchamp is something of a mentor to many young artists (and to would-be-eternally-young artists, your author included, who came of age in the 1960s) to whom he is affectionately 'Marcel.' Dada continues to be a source of inspiration for those who share its irreverent and anti-authoritarian spirit. The idea of the 'found object,' too, appeals to many artists who resist bringing one more non-biodegradable thing into a crowded world. Materials that already exist are increasingly used by artists who question or reject the attitude that art's worth lies in the process of crafting precious materials for aesthetic ends. Instead, art is defined by its function.

*　*　*

Allow me a personal note. Thinking about *dada* and Duchamp, I find myself considering a persistent question that is at the root of much Postmodern thinking. What matters --- a work's intention? or how it is used? I ponder this a lot, in relation to my art and others', and in response to things outside of art --- words, jokes, actions, images, inventions, tools.

What matters --- a thing's intention? or how it is used?

It seems to be a question worth asking all the time. Einstein probably asked it as he arrived at e=mc2. Willis Harmon wrote an entire book on *Higher Creativity* to consider the question.

Perhaps the answer is *Sometimes* and *Sometimes*.

Perhaps it is *Yes* and *Yes*.

CHAPTER THIRTEEN

MONDRIAN AND I

As Yugoslavia disintegrated into warring ethnic factions in the early 1990s, I made a small painting as a tribute to Mondrian, sadly titled *Nice Try, Piet...*

Every time I visit New York City, I try to set aside one day for a pilgrimage to the Museum of Modern Art. Early in the morning I start a long slow walk up Fifth Avenue from Soho. I go alone so I can stop anywhere along the way to browse through shops, get coffee, or people-watch at Rockefeller Center. I almost always see Someone Famous; once a network news anchor careened around the corner across from her office at NBC --- I was window-shopping at Tiffany's --- and crashed into me with her dry cleaning. I almost always witness some sort of urban crisis: fire engines or squad cars, parades or protests. It is most often Spring, always noisy, lively, energetic, and I love New York that day. Life, as I make my ritual stroll, is good.

At the museum I see whatever special shows interest me, and then I escalate up to the permanent collection. I suppose there was a time years ago that I went from painting to painting in a methodical way, but now my habit is different. I stand in the center of each room and make a slow turn, letting paintings invite me to them for a closer look. I seriously study whatever artwork lures my attention, and at the same time I make a mental note of what appeals to me in a new and different way on each visit. One day I was attracted to a gem of a painting by Matisse that I had never noticed before, one that I wasn't familiar with from reproductions (looking at a souvenir postcard of the *View of Notre Dame*, I have to admit that this subtle painting isn't well-served by reproduction; see chapter 5). Another time I spent several minutes exploring in close-up detail a series of large vertical paintings by Kandinsky, falling in love with passages of line and color. Every visit to the museum becomes a wonderful exercise in discovery --- about art, of course, but also about whatever it is that draws me to a certain work of art at a certain point in time.

In early 1991 I was at MOMA, doing 'my thing,' and I entered the small room hung with compositions by Piet Mondrian. A dozen or so paintings of varying sizes, squares and rectangles, verticals and diagonals, bore evidence to Mondrian's commitment to the integration of black, white, red, yellow and blue. These works weren't new to me; I had long admired Mondrian and used him as an example to students in design classes. But on this particular day, in a room I had passed through many times, I Got It. Here I was, a serious artist and teacher for over twenty years, and Mondrian's art was speaking to me for the first time in a truly profound way. I was so shaken, so moved, that I had to sit down. There is a bench in the room, and I was not alone as I sat and rather breathlessly looked at the paintings around the walls. Every now and then my eyes intersected those of people sitting nearby, people who looked as stunned as I felt. Our gazes momentarily met, and we nodded to each other ever so slightly. *Yes*, we were saying, *yes*, to each other and to Mondrian.

Later I met a friend-of-a-friend, an artist who asked about my day at the museum. I reviewed for him: so-and-so's work was terrific, and someone-or-the-other had a great installation. Then I cautiously began, "But you know, I had a really significant experience there..." and before I could go on, he interrupted excitedly: "Mondrian, right?" What was going on? we wondered. Why were we being so affected by work that hadn't stirred us this powerfully before?

For months afterwards, back at home in the provinces, I thought more and more about this episode. I investigated Mondrian with a good bit of seriousness, examining books of his paintings and reading his statements. I discovered that he was a Theosophist and made a mental note to look into what that might mean to his work; someday I will. It isn't hard to see what the artist was doing in a formal sense as he brought equivalent and exclusive elements together into balanced order. This is the stuff of any basic design class, and Mondrian's balanced grids exemplify the goals of composition in an elemental way.

But Mondrian's achievement as an artist goes much deeper than simple two-dimensional design. In the 1930s and '40s, Mondrian was developing his aesthetic language of line, shape and color along with other Modernists who were breaking with the pictorial tradition that had defined art since the Renaissance. Gone was illusionistic space, imitative form, and ultimately all reference to pictorial reality. In its place, artists used a universal language of pure form, freed from the constraints of subject matter and symbol.

This was profoundly heady stuff, philosophical, spiritual and, yes, political. Representational art of the time was being used by the extremes of the political right and left: the Mexican muralists, the American Social Realists, regionalists and nationalists pictured and proselytized from both sides of the political spectrum. Modernists like Mondrian were idealistic and anti-nationalistic; their pure visual language appealed to the universal and utopian. Modernist abstraction, says critic Arthur Danto, "set out to change the world and redeem the human spirit."

Over the years, working first from closely observed nature, Piet Mondrian discovered that he was interested solely in relationships. In his words, his goal was to achieve "pure reality" which he defined as "equilibrium through the balance of unequal but equivalent opposites." He pared his formal vocabulary down to painting's purest elements: red, yellow, blue, black and white *are* color. Each is completely independent of the other and yet each is necessary for color's completeness. To unify these oppositional elements, Mondrian limited his shapes to the single yet infinitely varied rectangle and introduced a structure of black lines to hold these forces in a state of tension and coherence.

Imagine doing what Mondrian did, time after time in painting after painting. Confronting the empty canvas, he set out to bring disparate elements into completeness, wholeness, and balance. If it can be done on the picture plane, the art implies, so can it be done in the world. Over and over Mondrian faced the blank canvas. What daring, what courage, what an act of faith! His painting process became a devotional act, a "bringing into being" of unity, relationship and meaning.

Art isn't made in a vacuum...What we feel compelled to do, whether it's making art or giving your life to God --- I personally don't think there's any difference between the two --- evolves out of the inner fabric of our lives...The work, the vocation is an attempt...to fulfill in an inner way, in a symbolic way, what the outer world is failing to provide...in the service of wholeness.

(Gail Godwin, *The Good Husband*)

I remember a day in late 1990, listening to the radio in the kitchen as the Berlin Wall came down. I stopped mid-chore and paid attention with great emotion and prayer-like intensity. There followed a period of weeks, perhaps months, when people like I who yearned for, spoke out for, and worked for the resolution of differences and the breaking down of barriers felt a surge of hope.

In retrospect it seems incredibly naive and simplistic, but as I visited New York City, I was still experiencing that sense of hopeful idealism. And when I walked into Mondrian's room at the Museum of Modern Art, the intention of his work connected with whatever was going on in my psyche. At that moment, through his art, the artist's intention and mine were aligned; we were on the same wave length. I Got It.

Many times art is hard to Get. It may take, as it did with Mondrian and me, many years; sometimes we never Get It. But oh, when it happens... Art has the power to connect us to some fundamental truth, to bring us to a place where idea and intention and form coincide. It is a revelation and an affirmation of something most profoundly divine and most essentially human.

> *The beauty of art and nature is a manifestation of the unity of being... It is to this wholeness that all orders of creation aspire, and from it that all have been created.*　　(Plotinus)

CHAPTER FOURTEEN

ART AND CONTEXT

Many artists continue to use the painting process to tap into the unconscious mind and to release primal impulses. This example is an amalgam of paintings by several heirs to Abstract Expressionism.

Context can be everything.

The gap between art and audience widened with Abstract Expressionism, the dominant art movement of the 1950s. It is a fact that whenever I first project a slide of a painting by Jackson Pollock, I hear grumbles of annoyance and see eyes rolling and heads wagging. Divorced from context, the personal, private and audacious visual language of Abstract Expressionism can be awfully hard to Get.

A good bit of history is necessary. The founders of Abstract Expressionism, which would become America's first major contribution to the tradition of Western art, came of age in the 1930s when American painting and sculpture were provincial, illustrational, and often used for political ends. As early as 1940 the Federation of American Painters and Sculptors rejected the figurative art of the time: "We condemn artistic nationalism which negates the world tradition of art at the base of modern movements."

In a 1943 catalog statement for the American Modern Artists show at the Riverside Museum in New York City, painter Barnett Newman declared the exhibition to be "a first step to free the artist from the stifling control of an outmoded politics." The new art, he stated, must oppose social realism and academic art; it must be anti-isolationist, anti-regionalist, anti-communist, and pro-internationalist. In the mid-1940s, Pollock declared: "The idea of an isolated American painting, so popular in this country during the thirties, seems absurd to me, just as the idea of creating a purely American mathematics or physics would seem absurd." And Robert Motherwell concurred in 1946: "Art is not national... To fail to overcome one's initial environment is never to reach the human." At the same time, Arthur Schlesinger's best-selling book *The Vital Center* expressed a kindred attitude from the viewpoint of political science.

Sometimes the very art that *appears* to be the simplest --- Mondrian's reductive grids, for example --- is necessarily simple because of the complexity of its content. Sometimes the art that *appears* to be the least political --- Abstract Expressionism --- is superficially misleading. The early Abstract Expressionists demanded a new art that was large and therefore unequivocal; that was abstract and unable to be "the plaything of politicians"; that was flat, in order to destroy illusion and to reveal truth; that spoke to the tragic and timeless "in kinship with primitives and archaic art."

Subsequent generations of Abstract Expressionists took this bold new style as license for free expression devoid of sociopolitical content, but the movement's originators made their art as a critique of the failure of both socialist and capitalist states. Abstract Expressionism was created to reject painting as a consumable commodity and propaganda; the style confronted the possibility of the free individual in modern society. In the act of painting, the artist-as-individual was fully free (and, it is important to add, fully responsible).

Novelist Don DeLillo's essay on writing and writers applies just as surely to the visual arts and artists:

> *Writing is a form of personal freedom. It frees us from the mass identity we see in the making all around us. In the end, writers will write not to be outlaw heroes of some underculture but mainly to save themselves, to survive as individuals.*

This chapter is full of quotations for a purpose. Primary sources --- the artists' own statements of their intent --- offer the best proof of Abstract Expressionism's relevance to the time that produced it. In many ways, the era *necessitated* the art. We have seen how art reflects the goals and values of the culture that produces it, but in the case of Abstract Expressionism art took a resistant and oppositional relationship to the Cold War conformity of the 1950s. While written words were being censored and people censured, it was only through the less literal vocabularies of abstract painting and music that individual voices could speak honestly and without fear. The resulting art forms --- Abstract Expressionism and improvisational jazz --- are by definition the most democratic forms of expression. They are spontaneous and beyond censorship, universal and at the same time truly American in their direct and vigorous spirit. This art is *free*.

> *Every new aesthetic reality makes one's experience even more*
> *private; and this kind of privacy... can in itself turn out to be, if*
> *not a guarantee, then a form of defense, against enslavement.*
> (Harold Brodsky)

It is a shame that Abstract Expressionism, with its noteworthy history and commendable intention, is frequently misunderstood. This style may mark the point where art veered farther away from public consciousness and acceptance, alienating audiences and providing a basis for some harmful myths about art and artists. Even in a serious study of art history, Abstract Expressionism is often explained solely by its formal attributes: large scale, it breaks with the tradition of easel painting; it is 'overall' and spontaneous rather than consciously organized; it responds to the automatism of the Surrealists and celebrates the accidental; it is private, with its energy occurring between the artist and the painting rather than, or in addition to, the painting and the audience; it displays, in critic Clement Greenberg's term, "flugilineous flatness." In other words, Abstract Expressionism is all too often reduced to its stylistic devices as though style was its point rather than its means.

Considering art in relation to its social and political context can make all the difference to our entry into the meaning of a style that is otherwise off-putting or obscure. Context can be the key. In the case of Abstract Expressionism, understanding the context out of which it was born counteracts the myth of art as an unbridled expression of 'self,' a mere indulgence of self, and reconnects the art to the external world.

Is it a failure of Abstract Expressionism that many people miss its point or misread it? Let me suggest that the artist's responsibility is not to the audience but to the work of art and to Art which that work serves.

True, art often acts as a mirror for the culture that produces it, but Abstract Expressionism functioned quite differently. The mainstream culture of post-war America was conformist, with a code everyone understood: behave, respect authority, don't ask questions, obey the rules, inhibit your sexuality, control your emotions, suppress your individuality and 'fit in.' Abstract Expressionism confronted every one of these societal strictures, and by so doing anticipated what the culture at large would be doing a decade later. *Do your own thing, Let it all hang out,* and *If it feels good, do it,* became the battle cries of a generation that questioned authority and set in motion the social revolutions of the 1960s.

While art often reflects the culture, it also has the power to foretell. After all, the job of the artist is to pay attention and, through the artwork, to direct our attention. The artist serves as 'see-er," *seer.* It makes sense then that art on the cutting edge --- the *avant garde* --- can anticipate attitudes which may eventually reach critical mass and express themselves within the culture at large.

> *Perhaps the function of the artist... can be more clearly seen if we compare (artwork) to the work of the historian who communicates a pattern which was invisible to his subjects when they lived it, and unknown to his contemporaries before he shaped it.*
> (Lawrence Leshan and Henry Margenau, *Einstein's Space and Van Gogh's Sky*)

CHAPTER FIFTEEN

PENDULUM SWINGS II

Nature Mort, a large painting I made in the late 1980s as I bemoaned the commercialization of *everything,* substitutes a universal bar code for the traditional landscape that would have occupied the center of a Medieval tapestry.

When the pendulum swung, the art world's spotlight shifted from the internalized paintings of Abstract Expressionism to the upbeat and refreshingly overt imagery of Pop Art, the 'in' style of the 1960s. Pop Art centered around and in some ways predicted America's increasing culture of consumerism. Andy Warhol's unending rows of consumer goods and media portraits, with their emphasis on packaging, celebrity and hype, just get truer and truer.

In its 1995 Rapid Access® brochure, Primo Angeli, Inc., a San Francisco marketing firm, promoted a new approach to package design:

...Why not first develop finished looking packages with highly competitive brands and product names. Test and qualify them with consumers. Then, turn the most effective packages over to R&D. Ask them to make a product that fits the pre-tested, pre-approved package. ...The **RapidAccess™** *approach reverses the role packaging has played in marketing new products. Now used as a creative catalyst, ...<u>package design assists in determining what the product might be, rather than the product determining the package.</u>*

(my emphasis)

I rest my case...

CHAPTER SIXTEEN

ART NOW

Modernism is so *efficient*, so *neat*, moving along in a logical step-by-step response to whatever came before, a straight line, always progressing forward. In contrast, the Postmodern Period --- *now* --- defies a simple model and might be best defined by its characteristics. Postmodernism is pluralistic, with many ideas occurring simultaneously and with no dominant style. It is characterized by rapid change, globalism and decentralization. The dominant tradition of Western Civilization --- Eurocentric, white, male, Christian, heterosexual --- opens up to diverse and multi-cultural perspectives. Postmodernism is holistic rather than linear, and the notion of unending progress is seriously questioned if not rejected outright. The positive outcome of progress through technology is subject to debate, and the inevitability of progress is scrutinized.

In Postmodern art, new questions require new ways of exploration. Artists reach the end of style (painters arrive at either a blank canvas, in the classical tradition, or an endless, romantic celebration of *me, me, me*) and begin to use style as another choice, an expressive element. Freed from the limitations of style, Postmodern artists dissolve the boundaries between media: painting, sculpture, video and text combine and create new syntheses. Art becomes an event, it is performed, and the viewer interacts with it and activates it. New media and techniques abound: sound, light, video, electronics, the 'virtual world.'

Some Postmodern art is anti-Modernist; full of cynicism, it decries meaning and reflects an aspect of the contemporary psychological condition. But much of the 'new,' while offering a necessary assessment of Modernism, is the next logical (inevitable?) step in that tradition; it opens up the forms, media and functions of art to new possibilities of meaning and hope.

Particular questions and issues compel Postmodern artists:

In a world of simulation, can originality exist?

The Postmodern artist appropriates styles from the past, borrowing imagery from media sources and combining information from high and low culture, to create multi-layered pastiches of shapes, signs, and images which effect multiple and contradictory interpretations.

Whose is the voice of authority? Who authors what we accept as 'truth'?

The Postmodern artist simulates and manipulates imagery, deconstructs and critiques history and 'the news,' explores point of view, decodes texts and subtexts, and reveals bias and conflicting agendas.

In an image-saturated culture, how does imagery work? Who and what determine and control the images that determine and control our attitudes and behavior? Postmodern artists confront the politics of representation. They comment on gender, race and sexual orientation.

The point is not to deposit your message in the other person's mind, but to somehow activate the layers of meaning already deposited there...   (Jay Rosen)

Postmodern art embodies the contemporary culture. It directs our attention to environmental concerns, to the growth and concentration of corporate power, and to urgent issues such as AIDS, homelessness and violence. Its exposes institutional and individual injustice, hypocrisy, myths and lies. Art continues to give a voice to the marginalized, to proclaim what no one dares to whisper, and to expose what is hidden from our daily view.

AFTER WORDS

Approaching the end of each semester, I remind myself that the goal of the course in Art Appreciation is exactly what its title states. The aim is not to *like* art, necessarily, or to understand every example of it, but to recognize that art has always been valuable and continues to be. The objective is to appreciate what art does. And, as we've seen, it does many things:

It celebrates. It acts as a mirror, a telescope, a microscope. It serves as an antidote, a forum, an invitation, a quest and a question, a possibility, a statement. It illuminates what is otherwise obscure. It provides a voice for those who are otherwise unheard. It asks important questions: Is meaning possible? Can art create meaning? Is the breaking down of barriers possible? Where should we draw the lines? Is the resolution of opposing forces possible? Is the sharing of power possible? Is authenticity possible?

> *The stupidity of people comes from having an answer for everything. The wisdom of (art) comes from having a question for everything.* (Milan Kundera)

The questions art dares to ask are ones we need to confront collectively and as individuals. We all have different jobs to take care of --- if you are an accountant, you spend your time being attentive to numbers; if you are a physician, you are mindful of symptoms and solutions --- and the artist's job is to pay attention to crucial issues and to raise important questions. If the artist doesn't do it, who will?

In a 1919 essay, Piet Mondrian wrote that "the deepest purpose of painting has always been to give concrete existence through color and line, to the universe that reveals itself in contemplation." Contemporary science is confirming that to a great degree we create our own minds by the manner in which we use them; we build and reinforce neural connections and networks by what we see and hear, think and do. At the end of the twentieth century, I look at our children with their digital superiority and their ability to process multiple, rapid-fired, disconnected images in their eyes and minds at once. For all the possible good this new cerebral skill may hold for the future, I wonder if coming generations might have a diminished capacity for prolonged contemplation. And it is that critical requirement that art demands of us --- the calm of lengthy contemplation --- which may be rendered obsolete by incomprehension and inability.

Art will endure, of course, as long as human imagination, dreams, memory and desire exist. Aspects of art --- certain media, techniques and styles --- may prove to be outmoded and useless (painting has been struggling to justify its *raison d'etre* for the last hundred years), but Art itself will continue as long as there are questions worth asking. Art has the potential to give us what we 'want,' what we lack and most need to fulfill us. From the earliest cave paintings, this has always been Art's power: to bring possibilities into being, to create the world.

> *Worlds are made not only by what is said literally, but also by what is said metaphorically.* (Nelson Goodman)

As world-makers, artists face questions that challenge their sense of individual responsibility: What if art does in fact have the power to 'work'? What if it does indeed matter? And if you think it doesn't matter, why do you make it? (Perhaps we artists should re-think the advice we are given to believe in what we do; shouldn't we do what we believe in? Figuring out what one believes in is the hard part...) What if art made from cynicism adds mistrust to a world that cannot afford it? What if art that is inauthentic adds falseness and chaos to a world that cries out for stability and coherence?

Artists go into the studio seeking 'the point.' They entertain ideas and ask questions. Ideas and questions are free; they exist on an invisible plane that I imagine to be hovering over all our heads. Through the process of making art, artists enter into a non-normal state; they relinquish self-consciousness --- the assertion of *me* --- and as poet Wendell Berry says, they "participate in the creation." Through the creative process, artists engage in a dialogue with all artists who have gone before them and with all those who will follow. They open up a channel to ideas, to "the creation," to the Divine.

By making art --- not for the sake of pleasure, money, fame, or self-indulgence, but for Art's sake --- artists sustain Art and renew it. Art is an active force, and if it is not fed it will diminish and die, and we will all be impoverished. Because Art is not a one-way proposition. It feeds us back. It nourishes us. It helps us transform our minds and our world. It 'works.'

Teaching Art Appreciation semester after semester, year after year --- same classroom, same jokes, same lessons, same tests --- never fails me; it is always satisfying. As I increase the breadth and depth of my inquiry into Art's forms and functions, important art validates Art's importance and great art confirms Art's value. Art is one way, and an important way, we seek meaning and sense in a world that so often refutes meaningfulness. The more I teach about Art and learn from it, the more it continues to renew my faith in the possibility of meaning and to reward me with hope.

> *Hope is an orientation of the spirit, an orientation of the heart. It is not the conviction that something will turn out well, but the certainty that something makes sense, regardless of how it turns out. Any body of thought that is in touch with reality, religious or otherwise, operates out of this orientation.*
>
> (Vaclav Havel)

At the end of a course in Art Appreciation, when all is said and done, I catch myself thinking that art is the *only* important thing. Deep down I know that we Get It in many ways and that art is just one of many necessary paths that lead us toward 'the point': musicians aim for it, prayer and meditation will get you there, poets and yogis do it.

Planting a field out of love for the earth or holding a dying person's hand, whatever we do in acts grand and modest to forge meaningful connections between us and beyond us --- these seem like the holiest things a person can do. It's what artists do. Striving toward the vital center, bringing the bubble into balance at a point where we stop and know... *it's true...*

That's what Art does.

I appreciate it.

SOURCES AND RESOURCES

The following textbooks contain reproductions of many of the artworks mentioned in this volume, as well as useful supplementary information about various styles, media and techniques.

History of Modern Art, by H. H. Arnason; Prentice Hall, Abrams.

Experiencing Art Around Us, by Thomas Buser; West Publishing.

Mainstreams of Modern Art, by John Canaday; Holt, Rinehart and Winston Inc.

Varieties of Visual Experience, by Edmund Burke Feldman; Prentice Hall, Abrams.

Understanding Art, by Lois Fichner-Rather, Prentice Hall.

The Creative Impulse, by Dennis J. Sporre; Prentice Hall.

Living with Art, by Rita Gilbert; McGraw Hill.

The Story of Art, by E. H. Gombrich; Prentice Hall.

Artist and Audience, by Terence Grieder; Holt, Rinehart and Winston Inc.

ART: A History of Painting, Sculpture, Architecture, by Frederick Hartt; Prentice Hall, Abrams.

Art: Context and Criticism, by John Kissick; Brown and Benchmark, Wm. C. Brown Communication.

Art: The Way It Is, by John Adkins Richardson; Prentice Hall, Abrams.

Art in the World, by Stella Dandell Russell; Holt, Rinehart and Winston Inc.

A World of Art, by Henry M. Sayre; Prentice Hall.

Modern Art, by Meyer Shapiro; George Braziller.

Art of the Western World, by Michael Wood, Bruce Cole and Adelheid Gealt; Summit Books.

History of Art , History of Modern Art, by H. W. Janson; Prentice Hall, Abrams.

SOURCES

The Postmodern idea of "appropriation" is old news to anyone who has ever taught. Teaching requires being constantly mindful of the subject(s) while doing all sorts of things --- scanning magazines in a dentist's waiting room, watching movies, reading novels --- so that one can glean information and examples from any and every sort of source. I have tried to acknowledge sources throughout this book, and to give credit when it is due, but some of my sources are now so much a part of what I teach and how I think that I am quite sure many go unrecognized. For example, my mother sent me Vaclev Havel's statement on hope, written on a scrap of paper in her own hand; I posted it in my studio for years and read it often before including it in my text. I have no idea when or where the statement was first said or first published. Some of the sources which have influenced my learning and teaching and which I recommend as supplements for *Getting It* include:

Ways of Seeing, by John Berger, Penguin Books.

A Life of One's Own, by Joanna Fields, J. P. Tarcher, Inc.

Philosophies of Art and Beauty, edited by Albert Hofstadter and Richard Kuhns, Random House.

Artists on Art, edited by Robert Goldwater and Marco Treves, Pantheon Books, (Random House).

Higher Creativity: Liberating the Unconscious for Breakthrough Insights, by Willis Harmon with Howard Rheingold, Jeremy Tarcher.

Meaning in the Visual Arts, by Erwin Panofsky, University of Chicago Press.

The Banquet Years, by Roger Shattuck, Vintage Books.

The Vital Center: The Politics of Freedom, by Arthur M. Schlesinger, Jr., Da Capo Press.

Abstract Expressionist Painting in America, by William C. Seitz, Harvard University Press.

How New York Stole the Idea of Abstract Expressionism, Freedom, and the Cold War, by Serge Guilbaut, University of Chicago.

The Bride and the Bachelors, by Calvin Tomkins, Penguin Books.

The Shock of the New, by Robert Hughes, Knopf, Random House.

Has Modernism Failed?, by Suzi Gablik, Thames and Hudson.

Bodies, Rest and Motion, 1993, New Line Home Video, Los Angeles.

ACKNOWLEDGMENTS

Many people have provided assistance and support for this project, and I am grateful to them: early readers and true friends Karen Houston and Emily Clark; Houghton Mifflin editors Cyndi Eller and Cindy Graff Cohen who "got it", and Elin Goldman who completed the process; Jim and Mary Hendrick, whose interest never flagged; and Ray Parish who is my pace-setter and beloved life partner. Above all, I appreciate the intelligence, curiosity and enthusiasm of the many students I have been privileged to teach over the years, most recently at El Paso Community College, who inspired, challenged and rewarded me on a daily basis.

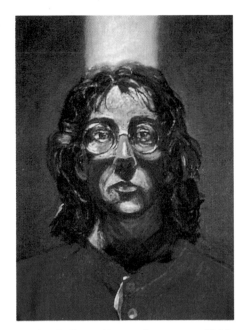

Self with Grace Descending   *1996*

Artist Becky Hendrick lives in La Union, New Mexico, where she and her husband, sculptor Willie Ray Parish, grow peaches and host the Border Art Residency.